AFRICAN WRITERS SERIES

Pothide[illegible]

✱ Four colour tra[illegible]
* Short Stories
† Poetry
‡ Plays
§ Biography/Poli[illegible]

PETER ABRAHAMS
✱ *Mine Boy*

CHINUA ACHEBE
✱ *Things Fall Apart*
✱ *No Longer at Ease*
✱ *Arrow of God*
✱ *A Man of the People*
✱ *Anthills of the Savannah*
100 *Girls at War**
120 *Beware Soul Brother*†

THOMAS AKARE
241 *The Slums*

T. M. ALUKO
70 *Chief, the Honourable Minister*

ELECHI AMADI
✱ *The Concubine*
44 *The Great Ponds*
210 *The Slave*
✱ *Estrangement*

I. N. C. ANIEBO
206 *The Journey Within*

KOFI ANYIDOHO
261 *A Harvest of Our Dreams*†

AYI KWEI ARMAH
✱ *The Beautyful Ones Are Not Yet Born*
154 *Fragments*
155 *Why Are We So Blest?*
194 *The Healers*
218 *Two Thousand Seasons*

BEDIAKO ASARE
59 *Rebel*

KOFI AWOONOR
108 *This Earth, My Brother*

MARIAMA BÅ
✱ *So Long a Letter*

MONGO BETI
13 *Mission to Kala*
77 *King Lazarus*
88 *The Poor Christ of Bomba*
181 *Perpetua and the Habit of Unhappiness*
214 *Remember Ruben*

STEVE BIKO
✱ *I Write What I Like*§

OKOT P'BITEK
193 *Hare and Hornbill**
266 *Song of Lawino & Song of Ocol*†

DENNIS BRUTUS
115 *A Simple Lust*†
208 *Stubborn Hope*†

SYL CHENEY-COKER
221 *The Graveyard Also Has Teeth*

DRISS CHRAIBI
79 *Heirs to the Past*

WILLIAM CONTON
12 *The African*

BERNARD B. DADIE
87 *Climbié*

MODIKWE DIKOBE
124 *The Marabi Dance*

MBELLA SONNE DIPOKO
57 *Because of Women*

AMU DJOLETO
41 *The Strange Man*
161 *Money Galore*

T. OBINKARAM ECHEWA
✱ *The Crippled Dancer*

CYPRIAN EKWENSI
2 *Burning Grass*
9 *Lokotown**
84 *Beautiful Feathers*
185 *Survive the Peace*
✱ *Jagua Nana*

BUCHI EMECHETA
✱ *The Joys of Motherhood*

OLAUDAH EQUIANO
10 *Equiano's Travels*§

NURUDDIN FARAH
252 *Sardines*

NADINE GORDIMER
177 *Some Monday for Sure**

BESSIE HEAD
✱ *Maru*
✱ *A Question of Power*
✱ *When Rain Clouds Gather*
182 *The Collector of Treasures**
220 *Serowe: Village of the Rain Wind*§

LUIS BERNARDO HONWANA
60 *We Killed Mangy-Dog**

OBOTUNDE IJIMÈRE
18 *The Imprisonment of Obatala*‡

EDDIE IROH
189 *Forty-Eight Guns for the General*

KENJO JUMBAM
231 *The White Man of God*

CHEIKH HAMIDOU KANE
119 *Ambiguous Adventure*

FARIDA KARODIA
✱ *Coming Home and Other Stories**

AHMADOU KOUROUMA
239 *The Suns of Independence*

MAZISI KUNENE
211 *Emperor Shaka the Great*†

ALEX LA GUMA
✱ *A Walk in the Night**
110 *In the Fog of the Seasons End*
✱ *Time of the Butcherbird*

DORIS LESSING
131 *The Grass is Singing*

HUGH LEWIN
251 *Bandiet*

HENRI LOPES
✱ *Tribaliks*

NELSON MANDELA
✱ *No Easy Walk to Freedom*§

JACK MAPANJE
236 *Of Chameleons and Gods*†

DAMBUDZO MARECHERA
207 *The House of Hunger**
237 *Black Sunlight*

ALI A MAZRUI
97 *The Trial of Christopher Okigbo*

TOM MBOYA
81 *The Challenge of Nationhood (Speeches)*§

THOMAS MOFOLO
229 *Chaka*

DOMINIC MULAISHO
204 *The Smoke that Thunders*

JOHN MUNONYE
21 *The Only Son*
45 *Obi*
94 *Oil Man of Obange*
153 *A Dancer of Fortune*
195 *Bridge to a Wedding*

MEJA MWANGI
143 *Kill Me Quick*
176 *Going Down River Road*

JOHN NAGENDA
✱ *The Seasons of Thomas Tebo*

The Trial of Dedan Kimathi

Ngugi wa Thiong'o
and
Micere Githae Mugo

HEINEMANN

Heinemann International
a division of Heinemann Educational Books Ltd
Halley Court, Jordan Hill, Oxford OX2 8EJ

Heinemann Educational Books Inc
361 Hanover Street, Portsmouth, New Hampshire, 03801, USA

Heinemann Educational Books (Nigeria) Ltd
PMB 5205, Ibadan
Heinemann Kenya Ltd
Kijabe Street, PO Box 45314, Nairobi
Heinemann Educational Boleswa
PO Box 10103, Village Post Office, Gaborone, Botswana
Heinemann Publishers (Caribbean) Ltd
175 Mountain View Avenue, Kingston 6, Jamaica

LONDON EDINBURGH MELBOURNE SYDNEY
AUCKLAND SINGAPORE MADRID
ATHENS BOLOGNA HARARE

ISBN 0-435-90191-5

Printed in Great Britain by
Cox & Wyman Ltd, Reading, Berkshire

90 91 92 93 94 95 10 9 8

PREFACE

August 1971 was the first time that we were sitting together arguing out many issues since our undergraduate days at Makerere of the early 60's where we used to share many literary interests including editing *Penpoint*, reading and directing plays. By this time both of us had already lived in North America and travelled in western Europe. Having encountered capitalism in its home ground, we were completely convinced that Imperialism was the enemy of all working peoples. There was America, for instance, with her huge highways, skyscrapers, the world's most efficient systems of communications, tremendous leaps in science and technology, every kind of material luxury one could think of, and yet, in the midst of these achievements, was the appalling poverty of workers especially those in the black and Puerto Rican Ghettos. All the advantages of modern science and technology, the wealth produced by the labour power of many people, went to the hands of a few. Amidst these were also the Indian reservations while abroad, were the giant American Imperialist projects of theft through deception, murder and enslavement of the people of Africa, Asia and Latin America. There was the American direct occupation of Vietnam and South Korea: there was the indirect American control of South Africa and Palestine. Truly, America's immense wealth was gained through the impoverishment and misery of millions!

We discussed the Vietnamese people's struggle against American Imperialism. They would surely win, we said. This led us back to Mau Mau, the actual subject of our discussion: was the theme of Mau Mau struggles exhausted in our literature? Had this heroic peasant armed struggle against the British Forces of occupation been adequately treated in our literature? Why was Kenyan Literature on the whole so submissive and hardly depicted the people, the masses, as capable of making and changing history? Take the heroes and heroines of our history: Kimathi, Koitalel, Me Kitilili, Mary Nyanjiru, Waiyaki. Why were our imaginative artists not singing songs of praise to these and their epic deeds of resistance? Whose history and whose deeds were the historians and creative writers recording for our children to read?

There was no single historical work written by a Kenyan telling of the grandeur of the heroic resistance of Kenyan people fighting foreign forces of exploitation and domination, a resistance movement whose history goes back to the 15th and 16th centuries when Kenyans and other East African people first took up arms against European colonial power—the Portuguese forces of conquest, murder and plunder. Our historians, our political scientists, and even some of our literary figures, were too busy spewing out, elaborating and trying to document the same colonial myths which had it that Kenyan people traditionally wandered aimlessly from place to place engaging in purposeless warfare; that the people readily accommodated themselves to the British forces of occupation! For whose benefit were these intellectuals writing? Unashamedly, some were outright defenders of Imperialism and lauded the pronouncements of colonial governors, basking in the sunshine of their pax-Anglo-Africana Commonwealths.

So why not a play on these neglected heroes and heroines of the Kenyan masses? Kimathi for instance? Yes. We agreed. We would co-author a play on Kimathi and later on Koitalel and Me Kitilili! But how were we to do it with one of us in Nairobi and the other in New Brunswick? We would try co-authoring through correspondence. This turned out to be too unrealistic, what with the distance and other commitments. It was not in fact until 1974, when we were already colleagues in the Department of Literature, University of Nairobi, that our dreams of 1971 materialised.

The writing of *The Trial of Dedan Kimathi* has been both challenging and exciting. It has put us through a lot of education in connection with the continuing struggle against economic and other forms of oppression. We also discovered that Kimathi was still a hero of the Kenyan masses. One day, for instance, we visited Kimathi's birthplace (thanks to Mr. Mundia who organised the trip) with the aim of eliciting a firsthand assessment of Kimathi from the people who had known him as a child, a villager and a guerrilla hero. It was a Sunday. The drive to Karunaini took us through beautiful valleys, ridges, hills and forests that helped the imagination recapture the countryside where the Mau Mau War was hottest and had often been fought out in pitched battles. Standing powerful and dominant to the north was Kirinyaga, the mountain at the foot of which the undulating Nyeri plains spread, rising to the Nyandarua mountains. Karunaini was right next to Nyandarua Forest and, standing very near the school where Kimathi once taught, we could see the spot where he was finally shot down. The huge trench that the people were once forced to dig by the British forces so as to cut off the villages from the Forests was still visible.

Among the group that stopped by the roadside to talk to us was a woman, who had once been Kimathi's pupil at Karunaini Independent School, and some four or five older men, who had known Kimathi since childhood. Had we too come all the way to see where Kimathi was born? From them, we learnt a few factual stories as well as one or two conflicting legends about this great fighter. For instance, it is generally assumed that Kimathi fought in the Second 'World' War and people have tended to assume that that was where he learnt his military skills as well as his skills in making guns. Kimathi *never* fought in *that* war. He evolved his brilliant guerrilla tactics and his enormous organising capacity from the needs of the struggle. Karunaini people were proud of their son; they talked of him as a dedicated teacher, the committed organiser of a theatre group he named Gichamu, as a man with a tremendous sense of humour who could keep a whole house roaring with laughter. They talked of his warm personality and his love of people. He was clearly their beloved son, their respected leader and they talked of him as still being alive. 'Kimathi will never die', the woman said. 'But of course if you people have killed him, go and show us his grave!' She said this in a strange tone of voice, between defiance and bitterness, and for a minute we all kept quiet.

We went back to Nairobi, turning over the words of those who had known Kimathi; had they themselves not shown us where he was shot and captured? Had they not told us that Kimathi's mother, although still deranged, was once allowed to see him in prison? Had they not told us about Kimathi's last testimony to be smuggled out of prison—that the struggle for Kenya's total liberation from foreign domination and oppression should continue until the wealth and the land was returned to the people of Kenya? Why then the sudden hostility when one of us raised the question of Kimathi's death? But there was also fire and enthusiasm in our hearts. We would try and recreate the same great man of courage, of commitment to the people, as had been so graphically described to us by the people who had not known of our coming. An even more important spur was the realization that the war which Kimathi led was being waged with even greater vigour all over Africa and in all those parts of the world where Imperialism still enslaved the people and stole their wealth. It was crucial that all this be put together as one vision, stretching from the pre-colonial wars of resistance against European intrusion and European slavery, through the anti-colonial struggles for independence and democracy, to post-independence struggle against neo-colonialism. This would be in the spirit of the woman who told us that Kimathi would never die.

As source material, Karari Njama's *Mau Mau From Within* became a very invaluable guide. Here was a man who had fought and lived alongside Kimathi, giving us a completely different picture of Kimathi and the Mau Mau War from what colonial writers had left behind in their works, like Henderson's *The Hunt of Dedan Kimathi*, Huxley's *A Thing to Love*, Ruark's *Uhuru* and *Something of Value*, to name only the most obvious.

We agreed that the most important thing was for us to reconstruct imaginatively our history, envisioning the world of the Mau Mau and Kimathi in terms of the peasants' and workers' struggle before and after constitutional independence. The play is *not* a reproduction of the farcical 'trial' at Nyeri. It is rather an imaginative recreation and interpretation of the collective will of the Kenyan peasants and workers in their refusal to break under sixty years of colonial torture and ruthless oppression by the British ruling classes and their continued determination to resist exploitation, oppression and new forms of enslavement.

In this we believe that Kenyan Literature—indeed all African Literature, and its writers is on trial. We cannot stand on the fence We are either on the side of the people or on the side of imperialism. African Literature and African Writers are either fighting with the people or aiding imperialism and the class enemies of the people. We believe that good theatre is that which is on the side of the people, that which, without masking mistakes and weaknesses, gives people courage and urges them to higher resolves in their struggle for total liberation. So the challenge was to truly depict the masses (symbolised by Kimathi) in the only historically correct perspective: positively, heroically and as the true makers of history.

Ngugi wa Thiong'o
Micere Githae Mugo

Nairobi, August, 1976.

ACKNOWLEDGEMENTS

We would like to thank Karari Njama and the publishers of *Mau Mau From Within* for permission to quote his version of *The Song of Kimathi*. We would also like to point out that although the faults and the shortcomings in the play are entirely ours, the play is a result of a collective effort with many concerned people freely giving us their comments and suggestions most of which we did incorporate into the play. It is impossible to name all of them except to say their comments were offered in the spirit of patriotism and of their hatred of Imperialism.

Characters

KIMATHI wa WACHIURI

NJAMA
MATENJAGWO
MBARIA KAHIU   } *Generals*
KIMEMIA
OLE KISIO

WOMAN

BOY

GIRL

SHAW HENDERSON, *who could also be: Judge, Prosecutor, etc.*
WAITINA—*a white police officer or District Officer*

FIRST SOLDIER

JOHNNIE

SECOND SOLDIER

FIRST BRITISH SOLDIER

SECOND BRITISH SOLDIER

K.A.R. SOLDIERS

GUARDS

WARDER

SETTLER

OLD WHITE DAME

GAKUNIA, *alias* GATOTIA

PRIEST

BUSINESS EXECUTIVE

POLITICIAN

BANKERS—EUROPEAN, AFRICAN, ASIAN

HUNGU
MWENDANDA   } *Collaborators*
GATI
GACERU

WAMBARARIA

CROWD and 1st, 2nd, 3rd, 4th & 5th Guerilla Fighters.

1

Preliminary Notes

The atmosphere is tense and saturated with sadness, as if the whole land is in mourning. Events move at a tremendous speed; people act with a general sense of urgency, as if to compete with time which is running ahead of them.

The play is in three movements which should be viewed as a single movement. The action should on the whole be seen as breaking the barrier between formal and infinite time, so that past and future and present flow into one another. The scenes (street, cell, courtroom) should also flow into one another.

There is impersonation, merging of characters and reflection of history emphasizing the complexity, duality and interrelationships of people and events. A character like Shaw Henderson, for instance, can be played as a Judge-Prosecutor and member of the Special Branch. He is also the enemy-friend of the Africans.

OPENING

Courtroom. A white judge presides. Near him is seated a fat important-looking African clerk, fiddling nervously with papers. Kimathi, chained, is in the dock. Guarding him, Waitina—a European District-cum-police officer—and two African K.A.R. soldiers, heavily armed. The courtroom is overcrowded. Africans squeeze around one side, seated on rough benches. Whites occupy more comfortable seats on the opposite side.

Dead silence

JUDGE: Dedan Kimathi s/o Wachiuri, alias Prime Minister or Field Marshal, of no fixed address, you are charged that on the night of Sunday, October the 21st, 1956, at or near Ihururu in Nyeri District, you were found in possession of a firearm, namely a revolver, without a licence, contrary to section 89 of the penal code, which under Special Emergency Regulations constitutes a criminal offence. Guilty or not guilty?
    [*Kimathi remains silent, defiant*]
I may warn you that your silence could be construed as contempt of court, in which case I could order that you be sent for a certain term to jail.
    [*Kimathi remains silent. There is murmuring
    in court. Judge hammers on the bench*]
Silence in court! I'll repeat the charge. Dedan Kimathi, you are charged that on the night of Sunday, October the 21st, 1956, at or near Ihururu in Nyeri District, you were found in possession of a firearm, namely a revolver, without a licence, contrary to section 89 of the penal code, which under Special Emergency Regulations constitutes a criminal offence. Guilty or not guilty?

    Silence for some seconds.
    Sudden darkness.

3

FIRST MOVEMENT

*Darkness reigns. Distant drums that grow louder and louder until
they culminate in a frantic, frenzied and intense climax, filling the
entire stage and auditorium with their rhythm. The intensity of
drumming eases up somewhat, to accommodate human voices.*

Twilight.

*Loud singing by a crowd of peasants. Their voices combine aggression
with firm determination. Note that the peasants singing should also
enact the flashback of Black people's History that follows the song.*

> Tutanyakua
> Mashamba yetu
> Tupiganie
> Uhuru wetu
> Natukomboe
> Elimu yetu
> Tutanyakua
> Viwanda vyetu
> Utamaduni
> Ni mashamba yetu
> Damu na jasho
> Zatiririka
> Tutakomboa
> Udongo wetu!

*A shot in the air. Overwhelming darkness. Drums and voices
fall silent. Through the silence cuts the chilling scream of a person,
followed by groans and more screams.*
*Whiplashes are heard falling on human skins. Another loud, agonis-
ing scream. Abrupt silence.*
*Vague twilight on part of the stage as drumbeats start a slow, mournful
movement. Sad music saturates the background as the enactment of
the Black Man's History takes place on the stage. The phases re-*

capitulated flow into one another, without break or interruption.

Phase I: An exchange between a rich-looking black chief and a white hungry-looking slave trader. Several strong black men and a few women are given away for a long, posh piece of cloth and a heap of trinkets.

Bereaved relations and children weep, throwing themselves onto the ground, while others raise closed fists in a threatening manner.

Phase II: A chain of exhausted slaves, roped onto one another, drag themselves through the auditorium, carrying heavy burdens, ending up on the stage. They row a boat across the stage, under heavy whipping.

Phase III: A labour force of blacks, toiling on a plantation under the supervision of a cruel, ruthless fellow black overseer. A white master comes around and inspects the work.

Phase IV: An angry procession of defiant blacks, chanting anti-imperialist slogans through songs and thunderous shouts:

LEADER: Away with oppression!
   Unchain the people!
CROWD: Away with oppression!
   Unchain the people!
SONG: Tutanyakua mashamba yetu!
   Tutakomboa Afrika yetu
   Tutanyakua viwanda vyetu!
LEADER: Away with exploitation!
   Unchain the people!
CROWD: Away with exploitation!
   Unchain the people!
LEADER: Away with human slaughter!
CROWD: Unchain the people!
LEADER: Brothers, we shall break—
CROWD: Exploiters' chains!
LEADER: Rally round the gun!

CROWD: Make a new earth!

SONG: Kupigwa na kufungwa jela
         Hakutatuzuia sisi wananchi
         Kunyakua Uhuru
         Na mashamba yetu.

Staccato burst of machine gunfire.
The drums respond with a deafening, rhythmic intensity.

FEW VOICES: Uhuruuuuuuu—uu!

Silence.

Now definite dawn breaks over the full stage, catching figures running across. Some of the running figures are in underwear. For a time, action focusses on two retreating Mau Mau guerillas with machine guns on the ready. Note that a bush is just visible. Also a few boulders by the road side. A few running figures escape through the auditorium.

Offstage we hear protesting voices and sounds of rough kicks, slaps and whiplashes.

Enter Waitina, with Gakunia—Gatotia, hooded

WAITINA: [*addressing two soldiers stationed at the opposite end of the stage*]: Askari, cover the streets well and shoot down at bloody terrorists. Sikia?
SECOND SOLDIER: Ndio Afande!

1st soldier shows no enthusiasm.

WAITINA: Askari!
SECOND SOLDIER: Fande!
WAITINA: Line up those Mau Mau villagers two by two.

6

SECOND SOLDIER: Tayari Bwana!

WAITINA: March them to the screening ground. He [*nodding at First Soldier*]: can guard the street. And tell him to wake up for Christ's sake! Sikia?

SECOND SOLDIER: Ndio Bwana.

Two rows of peasants now appear.
2nd Soldier tries in vain to make them march in step.

WAITINA: [*storming*]: March properly! Pesi! Na pana kimbia. Hands on your heads. Haraka! March on! [*2nd Soldier turns round and dashes back*]: Ngoja!

The people stop, looking confused but defiant, following Waitina's contradictory orders. A few more peasants are roughly pushed in by Second Soldier. They are brought before Waitina who pierces them with murderous eyes. Gakunia, the hooded collaborator, faces them.

WAITINA: Leta karatasi yako.

FIRST MAN: Sina.

WAITINA: [*kick*]: Sina Afande! Rudia!

FIRST MAN: Sina Afande.

WAITINA: Kazi yako?

FIRST MAN: Kulima.

WAITINA: Mtu ya Kimathi?

FIRST MAN: Hapana. [*Waitina raises his gun as if to hit him and remembering, the man quickly adds*]: Afande.

The hooded collaborator nods.

WAITINA: [*pushing the man roughly*]: Kwenda. You'll answer more questions at the screening yard, black bastard! . . . And you? [*Gakunia wags a hand at the next person—a man wearing a red shirt, carrying a basket with same fruits in it.*] No, not you. Wewe na shati nyekundu.

SECOND MAN: Mimi?

Waitina takes the basket from him roughly and peers inside it.

7

WAITINA: [*aggressively*]: Unafanya kazi wapi? What are you carrying?

SECOND MAN: I am a fruitseller. Matunda. I sing: "Oranges cheap today".

WAITINA: [*cannot help laughing at the man's antics. Then suddenly, he takes a few oranges and throws the basket away so that the rest of the fruits scatter.*]: Kwenda screening. Lazima you go to Manyani to sell your fruits there.

[*The man bites his fingers and makes frustrated grimaces. He tries to pick the basket and oranges but Waitina barks at him*]. Kwenda pesi! Wote march!

The whole line goes across the stage. As they march past, we should see the man still looking anxiously about him as if he had been expecting to see someone and his plans had been frustrated.

It is now proper daylight. A woman walks across the stage. She is between thirty and forty years of age, with a mature but youthful face, strongly built. Goodlooking. She wears a peasant woman's clothes and is barefoot. Though apparently a simple peasant, the woman is obviously world-wise, and perceptive of behaviour and society. Throughout, her actions are under control: her body and mind are fully alert.

Fearless determination and a spirit of daring is her character. She is versatile and full of energy in her responses to different roles and situations. A mother, a fighter, all in one. She wears a kanga cloth wrapped around her upper body— over her simple frock—and has a small kondo, a sisal basket, hanging over her neck and across the shoulder over her shawl on the side nearest the audience. She walks not exactly stealthily, but with great care—as if she treads on treacherous ground. She walks straight into the mouth of a gun.

WOMAN: Uuu—u! Nduri ici ni kii giki?

She moves backwards. The gun follows her. A white man, johnnie style, in green bush battledress, follows.

JOHNNIE: Simama kabisa! Good. Passbook.

WOMAN: Ati pasi?

JOHNNIE: Ndiyo, passbook. Wapi passbook?

WOMAN: Sina.

JOHNNIE: Sema Afande.

WOMAN: [*defiance in her tone.*] Afande.

JOHNNIE: Sina, Afande!

WOMAN: Sina Afande [*said with a saucy, sluggish tone suggesting,* "I don't have afande".]

JOHNNIE: Kuja, come here. [*She does not move. It is he who walks around her. She moves at such an angle that the kondo is slightly hidden from him. He looks her up and down. With the tip of his gun, he attempts to lift her skirt as if to see her legs. She brushes it aside disapprovingly, with dignity, and moves a step back. He stops moving and nods his head as if she has found favour in his eyes. Now a lascivious smile spreads over his face.*] Not bad. Nice legs, eh? Nice pretty face, eh?

[*He is about to relax and even be at ease with his gun when come a shout from offstage:*

"Laini!"—*a huge whiplash.* "Laini." *He quickly peers over his shoulders and resumes his former seriousness.*]

Why? Kwa nini wewe hapana passbook?

Where is your passbook?

WOMAN: Mimi? Women, they don't carry *passi*.

JOHNNIE: [*again appraises her. Relaxes. Nodding his head lasciviously*]: Women are their own passbooks, eh? Even to heaven. [*grinning seductively*]: Do you live around these parts? [*Suddenly, before she can answer, he becomes tense, obviously frightened. Gun ready. Moves a step or two away from her.*]

What, what's that? What's that bag you are carrying? [*hysterically*]: Toa! Toa! Weka chini, upesi!

WOMAN: This? [*showing the kondo with a casual, rather surprised air of pretended indifference.*]

JOHNNIE: Put it on the ground.

WOMAN: It's only a kondo, a small basket for women's work.

JOHNNIE: Pull it off, I say. That's good. Put it on the ground. Good.

9

Now, hands on your head. Move a step back. Two steps. That's good. Don't try any tricks now. [*He is moving towards the kondo, gingerly, but at the same time keeping a watchful eye on the woman.*]

WOMAN: [*She is also tense, but puts on the same air of casual indifference. To distract him, talks rather hurriedly.*]
Are you frightened? A white Bwana frightened by a woman's skirt? A woman's 'gardening' and 'market' basket?

JOHNNIE: [*picking up the basket*]: You never know what's hidden in these *shenzi* things.

Pours out the contents. The woman is tense but pretends otherwise. Bananas, oranges, sweets potatoes and parcel wrapped in paper fall out. Meanwhile, the woman is talking, cunningly trying to distract Johnnie.

WOMAN: Imagine. I would never have believed it.
A whiteman. A soldier. Afraid . . . .

JOHNNIE: Aaa, only bananas. . . .

WOMAN: I shall narrate this to the whole neighbourhood. . . .
[*Johnnie smiles at her. Takes a banana and peels it, taking it easy, obviously trying to hide his earlier fears*]: And eating bananas too. What a morning! What a day of wonders. [*a little mischievously*]: Can I remove my hands from my head?

JOHNNIE: Of course. A whiteman also gets hungry, especially after a whole night without sleep or food. Had to fight off those bloody terrorists until daybreak. This . . . [*Gobbles up another banana*]: this was only a precaution. Besides, you might have carried a gun. You look like a Mau Mau. Like one of them, Kimathi women. Wanjiru, they called her. She was lean, wiry and strong. Fought like a tiger in the battle of the Beehive. No wonder the terrorists made her a Colonel. [*somewhat forgetting himself*]: H'm. Should have seen when we captured her. She swore at us, spat in our faces and kicked like a wild goat as we bound her. Later at Karunaini camp, she would not eat or drink. And she would not tell us where we could find Kimathi. And you know? She bit my finger. And why? I wanted to see if she was really a woman. Our Africans: Gati, Hungu, Mwendanda and even Wambararia, Kimathi's brother, were frightened of her. [*He now takes the parcel and unwraps it. . . . The woman is talking fast*].

WOMAN: All the same. It's strange. Our men don't fear women. They are not frightened by . . . by . . . .

JOHNNIE: Aaah, just bread. Ha ha ha! [*on second thoughts after feeling it*]: Rather heavy bread, I must say. Bush millet, eh? Could have been a grenade. They are quite cunning, you know. Homemade guns. Homemade machine guns. Fanatics! Shall we have a bite?

He makes as if to break it into two. The woman dramatically kneels on the ground, almost reaching out for his legs. He is shocked and again frightened by this unexpected move. He moves back a step, puts the bread down and points the gun at her. She talks all the time.

WOMAN: [*simultaneously with the above action*]: Don't eat it. Bwana. Master. Afande a hundred times. It's all I have to quieten the enemy who is finishing us.

JOHNNIE: Enemy?

WOMAN: Hunger. If you take it, I'll die. I spent so many hours kneading the heavy millet paste. Look. You have almost finished all my bananas. You deserve to die. Have mercy on a poor woman.

JOHNNIE: [*Obviously relieved and pleased with her supplication and feminine submissiveness. He does not realize that she is over-reacting.*]
You don't look too poor to me. Stand up. All you need is a brush, water, soap, high heels. A modern lady.

WOMAN: Bwana, I'm only a poor woman. Leave me alone to go my own way. I am only a poor woman carrying food to save my dying children.

JOHNNIE: [*moving towards her, teasingly, as if to touch her*]: It is poor ones like you who carry food to them—Mau Mau in the forest, eh? [*the woman retreats*]: Where is your husband?

Before the woman can respond, there is a sudden noise of running footsteps without. Johnnie starts, panics momentarily, takes his gun and starts to run away. Remembering the woman, he turns back, gives a big knowing wink and then runs out. She makes some kind of obscene gesture at him, looks all around to detect the source of the noise and seeing no one appear, begins to collect bits of her scattered load. She puts the bread into her kondo first, collects the sweet potatoes and is in the process of collecting the oranges when she hears the voices of two KAR African soldiers who are walking in her direction. She grabs the scattered paper wrappings, a few more oranges and abandons the rest, rushing off to hide in the nearby bushes, just in time to avoid an encounter with the soldiers.

FIRST SOLDIER: [*anger and cynicism fused*]: Where are the terrorists who were supposed to be all over Nyeri? We've been patrolling all night without as much as catching sight of a single one of them. Simply harassing innocent villagers. The way mzungu makes us thirst to kill one another!

SECOND SOLDIER: [*irrelevantly. Viciously*]: The bloodyfuckin' Mau Mau are finished without that bugger Kimathi!

FIRST SOLDIER: What is the idea of arresting a whole village then?

SECOND SOLDIER: [*irritably*]: For screening. These natives are very slippery, man. They are the same people as attacked the homeguard post last night trying to release Kimathi. But they will see. Their bloody Kimathi is appearing in court at Nyeri today. This afternoon. He is going to get a proper court trial. Not like the jungle ones he used to stage in the forest. See how fair *mzungu* is?

FIRST SOLDIER: Ask me tomorrow if there is no attempt to rescue him. Something like what happened last night.

SECOND SOLDIER: Personally, I don't think they will try again. Mau Mau. . . . They are fuckin' cowards. They won't come out into the open in daylight and fight it out like men.

FIRST SOLDIER: Well, they have been known to do just that many times. If the government wants to avoid trouble, it should take precautions. Make sure that sympathizers remain as far as possible.

SECOND SOLDIER: I thought just now you were asking why the villagers had been taken prisoners?

FIRST SOLDIER: Being taken prisoner and being kept away are two different things.

SECOND SOLDIER: You think the mzungu is a fool. H'm. As we are talking now Gatotia, Gaceru, Gati, Mwendanda and Wambararia, Kimathi's own brother, are wearing hoods, pointing out the terrorists and their supporters one by one. I myself fear something quite different. Angry mothers who have lost their husbands and children might want to tear that beastly Kimathi to pieces!

FIRST SOLDIER: Wapi? That's what Bwana Shaw Henderson says. But he doesn't know the people. Kimathi is a hero to the people. They love him like anything, say what you will.

SECOND SOLDIER: [*suspiciously*]: You are talking like one of them, man.

FIRST SOLDIER: [*offended*]: What are you trying to say?

SECOND SOLDIER: [*trying to mend matters*]: Bloody bugger. [*slaps him on the shoulder*]: Don't be angry, man. A soldier's joke. But. . . let me tell you, after the trial, after Kimathi is hanged, there will be no more fighting. It will be the end of this bloody struggle. Mzungu! Don't play with him.

FIRST SOLDIER: Well, time will tell.

Offstage we hear the sound of jeeps and heavy vehicles revving their engines.

SECOND SOLDIER: Quick, the trucks are moving off. [*suddenly noticing the oranges on the ground*]: Look! A sign that Mau Mau are around.

FIRST SOLDIER: Don't other people eat oranges? Come on, let us catch the trucks before they take off.

[*They dash out in an exaggerated soldierly manner.*]

WOMAN: [*comes out of hiding*]: Wui, that was another narrow one. Escaping from the leopard's claws to fall into the lion's mouth. [*she begins to collect the remaining oranges*]: What was it one of those soldiers said? "The way the enemy makes us thirst to kill one another." How right he was! He must be one of the lost sons of the soil. H'm. Take the case of us peasants, for one. We are told you are Luo, you are Kalenjin, you are Kamba, you are Maasai, you are Kikuyu. You are a woman, you are a man, you are this, you are that, you are the other. [*after some thought*]: Yes. We are only ants trodden upon by heavy, merciless elephants.

Sad and shaking her head, the woman collects a stone to sit on from the edge of the stage, singing as she does so. She continues to arrange her possessions properly in the basket, wrapping the loaf with special care.

SONG: Bururi uyu witu Andu Airu
Ngai ni aturathimiire
Na akiuga tutikoima kuo
[*or any other appropriate song of struggle*]

Sound of an aeroplane overhead. Woman looks up. She continues with her task.

WOMAN: The trial of our strength
Our faith, our hopes, our resolve
The trial of loyalty
Our cause
I must find the fruitseller quickly
I must watch out for any more enemies' traps.

Finishes the wrapping up in a hurry. As she is about to start off, enter a youth—a big boy, nearing manhood and dressed roughly—chasing a girl. The girl is obviously very young but has undoubtedly seen life and hard times. The two run right across the stage. Then they come back. The boy catches the girl and both tumble on the floor. The boy, holding the girl roughly, is shouting.

BOY: Where is it?
Where is my money?
I will kill you for it.

Woman goes and separates them. She's obviously strong and holds them at arm's length on each side.

WOMAN: Shame on you. A big boy, well, a young man like you! And you want kill your sister! Your own mother's daughter!

BOY: Sister? She is not my sister. She is nobody's sister! She is a thief.

GIRL: I'm not a thief, you brute!

WOMAN: What has she done?

GIRL: Nothing . . . [*Sob*] . . . he . . . [*sob*] . . . just a big bully.

BOY: Nothing! [*struggling to free himself*]: Let me get at her and her *nothing* will turn into *something*.

WOMAN: [*in motherly anger*]: Or you will turn into nothing unless you become more human.

BOY: [*Incensed*]: A cheat. A slut. She must give me back my money. Else—else—

GIRL: Puuu. [*she spits. Boy tries to get at her. Woman holds him. But the girl breaks away and vanishes. He tries to follow her, but the woman holds him firmly.*]

BOY: [*really angry and hurt*]: You have now let her go. You are a bad woman. But I'll get her.

WOMAN: [*shaking him thoroughly*]: You are a woman's son? I have a mind to wring your neck. Running about and fighting like that when screeners and army jeeps are all over Nyeri. Where is your heart? Can't you see that you are big enough?

That you could easily be taken to Manyani? What has she done? [*lets him go. Then looks at him up and down intently. The boy is somewhat frightened*]: Haven't I seen you somewhere before?

BOY: [*pause during which Boy scrutinises the woman. Bitterness and fear intermingle, he involuntarily begins to tell his story*]: It was in Nairobi, you see. She and I and other boys and girls used to roam the streets together.

[*The boy hesitates, re-examines the woman and then looks down.*]

WOMAN: Don't be afraid now. Sit down here. Yes, you used to roam the streets. Which streets?

BOY: Eastleigh, Pumwani, Shauri Moyo, Bahati, Makadara and the centre of the city: Delamere Avenue, Hardinge, Kingsway, Queensway, Government Road—everywhere.

WOMAN: Yes?

BOY: [*beginning to enjoy his exploits and a sense of his own dangerousness*]: We scrounged into every dustbin from Kariobangi to Grogan Road. But mostly we'd hang around big hotels: New Stanley, Norfolk, Grosvenor. There were a lot of settlers and tourists and we would carry their bags. Sometimes we would act crippled or blind and deaf. They would give us money—some of them as much as *ten* shillings! The police would often come chasing us away, but we managed. Somehow. [*Pause.*]

WOMAN: Go on.

BOY: Then one day, myself and this girl were sitting outside New Stanley. As we were talking, a fat American came loaded with baggage [*becoming excited again*]:

"Saidia maskini, sah

Me and my sister

can carry your bags."

[*feigning the American's appearance and speech while unloading imagined baggage and giving it to imagined totos*]:

"Here, you take this, boy. And your sister can take this, okay? Good boy."

16

[*boy walks along pretending to be a tourist*]: A beauddiful
country ... a beauddiful ciddy ... and beauddiful people,
eh ?"
[*boy takes imagined camera off his shoulder and then clicks
photographs left, right and centre*]:
"Take the baggage to that taxi over there.
Understand ? Good."
[*boy moves a few more steps and then stops, wiping his sweat*]:
"Ahsonde soona" [*Gives ten shillings to imagined boy and girl.
At this juncture the boy stops acting tourist.*]

BOY: [*with fresh bitterness*]: I gave her the money to go to get change
while I waited for another American. She ran away. She never
came back. I looked for her in Nairobi but she always managed
to hide away from me. Nairobi is a big city, not like Nyeri—
a baby town. She disappeared. And then came the madness
mzungu called Operation Anvil and I was brought here.
Today by luck, I saw her.

WOMAN: So you decided to beat her ? And you would have killed
her because of five shillings—given you by a mzungu ?

BOY: I know people who have been killed for much less than that.

WOMAN: Shame on you! [*fixes him with an admonishing look ...
sudden realisation*]: I have been watching you ever since you
started your story and now I know I have seen you before.
You used to organize the group of boys who scouted for beer
brewers in Mathare Valley. Am I not right ?

BOY: [*eyeing the woman as if she were a prophet*]: How did you know ?
Were you in Nairobi too ? We called it the city of life and death.

WOMAN: [*the woman chuckles*]: Come. I'll give you the money you
were fighting for.

*He follows her. She takes her kondo, looks inside, then suddenly
seems to remember. She sits down and then from inside her
dress pulls out a tiny bag of money. She raises her head and
finds him looking at her, but he is actually gazing at the loaf of
bread.*

WOMAN: You are hungry, aren't you?

BOY: I have not eaten anything since yesterday.

WOMAN: Here. Take this twenty shillings. Go and buy yourself something to eat. And bring me the change. Right here.

BOY: [*taking the money unbelievingly*]: Thank you, Mama. Truly I thank you. [*dashes off the stage.*]

WOMAN: Ngai! It is the same old story. Everywhere. Mombasa. Nakuru. Kisumu. Eldoret. The same old story. Our people . . . tearing one another . . . and all because of the crumbs thrown at them by the exploiting foreigners. Our own food eaten and leftovers thrown to us—in our own land, where we should have the whole share. We buy wood from our own forests; sweat on our own soil for the profit of our oppressors. Kimathi's teaching is: unite, drive out the enemy and control your own riches, enjoy the fruit of your sweat.

It is for this that the enemy has captured him. [*boy returns, ravenously eating maandazi.*]

BOY: Here, your change. Thank you. [*he stands there, uncertainly.*]

WOMAN: Sit down and eat slowly. Nobody is going to steal it from you. If I were your mother, I would have you wash your filthy hands thoroughly, mend your clothes, wash them and teach you how to eat properly.

BOY: I have no mother.

WOMAN: You?

BOY: Yes. She died during childbirth.

WOMAN: And father?

BOY: Father was driven away from Mbari land in Nyeri by one of his relatives who worked as a court interpreter. Now that man is a big government chief and a big landowner. [*maliciously*]: But I will never forget the day Kimathi's men burnt down his homeguard post. That post used to be the people's grave!

WOMAN: And don't I now know the man you are talking about?

BOY: H'm. The man was clever at court cases and bribed the magistrates. Father and I went to Nairobi. He found a job with a firm of timber merchants. A tiny room: a tiny salary. Then I did not understand and I would steal from him, even the little that he earned for both of us. His ambition was to earn enough to come back to Nyeri and buy a piece of land. But he never made it. The machine cut off his right hand ... and ... he died of bleeding. No medical care from his employers. I was thrown out of the room he had rented.

WOMAN: It was hard for you then!

BOY: Aaa. Nairobi. I have fought with dogs and cats in the rubbish bins, for food. And I also remember this bakery. It belonged to an Indian. Periodically, he would throw away the rotten bread. We all ran for it. This pit is mine. This pipa is mine. Dogs, cats, girls, boys, all. But we also learnt how to live and we became men and women before our time.

WOMAN: [*thinking deeply. Sadly*]: Yes. I too have lived in the city. I know the life you have described. Fighting ... Drinking ... Fighting ... Drinking ... Kangari, karubu, busaa, chang'aa ... Mathare Valley ... Pumwani ... all that and more. I was a bad woman ... a lost stinking life ... until I heard the call.

BOY: The call? Of Jesus?

WOMAN: [*laughing*]: No. [*seriously*]: The call of our people. The humiliated, the injured, the insulted, the exploited, the submerged millions of labouring men and women of Kenya.

BOY: I don't understand.

WOMAN: [*impatiently*]: And you call yourself a man! What is it you don't understand? The things I talk about are written all over, written like large signs everywhere. [*pause*]: The day you understand why your father died: the day you ask yourself whether it was right for him to die so; the day you ask yourself: "What can I do so that another shall not be made to die under such grisly circumstances?" that day, my son, you'll become a man. Just now you are a beast and the girl was right to call you a brute. Here. Take these fifteen shillings and never you beat that girl again. [*makes as if to go*]:

BOY: But ... please ... don't go away ... I want to ask you something.

WOMAN: Quick. I have work ahead.

BOY: Just now, a few minutes ago, you gave me twenty shillings.

WOMAN: Yes.

BOY: You asked me to bring back your change.

WOMAN: Yes.

BOY: What made you think I would bring it back?

WOMAN: Weren't you beating a girl for not bringing you your change?

BOY: But mama!

WOMAN: Yes.

BOY: I want to confess. I wanted to run away with it all.

WOMAN: Why didn't you?

BOY: I don't know. I just came back.

WOMAN: I knew it. I knew you would return.

BOY: But mama!

WOMAN: Yes.

BOY: I don't know how to thank you for what you have done today. But . . . but . . . If I can do something, anything, you know . . . like cleaning up your house, your compound, weeding your shamba, even washing your clothes—

WOMAN: [*angry*]: You want to change masters! A black master for a white master! Have you no other horizon? Except to be a slave! If I didn't have better things to do, why, I would properly thrash you.

BOY: It is not that . . . I'm not afraid of work . . . any work.

WOMAN: [*She is about to go . . . then suddenly an idea strikes her. She looks at him closely, looks at her watch hidden in a pocket, then looks at him again*]: Would you really like to do some work? Are you ready for a job—no, a task? Are you ready to become a man?

BOY: [*proudly, enthusiastically*]: I am.

WOMAN: Ready for initiation?

BOY: [*offended*]: Why do you doubt me? Give me any task, anywhere.

WOMAN: Listen carefully. Dedan Kimathi has been captured.

BOY: So they say. But is it true what they also say?

WOMAN: What?

BOY: [*becoming really excited*]: They say . . . they say he used to talk with God.

WOMAN: Yes. The fighting god in us—the oppressed ones.

BOY: They say . . . they say that he could crawl on his belly for ten miles or more.

WOMAN: He had to be strong—for us—because of us Kenyan people.

BOY: They say . . . they say that he could change himself into a bird, an aeroplane, wind, anything?

WOMAN: Faith in a cause can work miracles.

BOY: They say . . . they say that the tree under which he used to pray fell to the ground?

WOMAN: There are people, my child, with blessed blood. And when something happens to them, the wind and the rain and the sun will tell. Even hyenas. Their death can shake mountains and give life to the volcanoes long thought to be dormant.

BOY: Maybe they only captured his shadow, his outer form . . . don't you think? . . . and let his spirit abroad, in arms.

WOMAN: Your words contain wisdom, son. Kimathi was never alone . . . will never be alone. No bullet can kill him for as long as women continue to bear children. [*with even greater conviction*]: Let a thousand bullets be shot through our heads, but this I believe: one day, the soil will be restored to the people. Our land *shall* one day be truly ours. [*pause*] But listen, there is an urgent task to be done. Kimathi is appearing in court to-day. This afternoon. Would you like to run a mission for Kimathi?

BOY: My life: what would I not give?

WOMAN: Talking is easy. It is deeds that show a man.

BOY: I am ready.

WOMAN: Do you know where the courtroom is in town?

BOY: Not far from the remand prison, near the Native Council.

WOMAN: Just so. There, outside the prison gates or outside the courtroom, or somewhere between the prison gates and the courtroom, you will find a man selling oranges. He will be wearing a red shirt. He will be singing: "Oranges cheap to-day! Thandaraita —aaa." Give him this loaf of bread.

BOY: [*disappointed*]: Only this?

21

WOMAN: Bread is life!

BOY: Bread for Dedan?

WOMAN: You be careful. Very very careful. What you are carrying is worth a life. You hear?

BOY: But bread. Only bread.

WOMAN: Yes. Guard it with your life. I'll be watching you. Go well. Watch every step you take.

[*she goes out.*]

BOY: Dedan. Kimathi. Bread. Trial. It cannot be! IT CAN NOT BE! [*seized by sudden thought*]: Mama! Mama! [*he runs after her, but too late*]: Oh, she has gone now. And she would not tell me her name. Or where I could find her later.

Stands rooted at the spot as a whisper breaks through the air.

WOMAN'S VOICE: The day you'll ask yourself . . . what can I do so that another shall not die under such grisly circumstances . . . that day you'll become a man, my son.

BOY: The Trial of Dedan Kimathi. I must be there to hear it. [*exit*]

SECOND MOVEMENT

Street

A street outside the court. Quite a big crowd has gathered around. The woman, disguised as a man in a red shirt, is selling oranges from a basket 'he' is carrying.

FRUITSELLER: Oranges cheap today
Oranges cheap today
On your way to heaven,
You gonna get an orange.

People walking by stop to see the shrill-voiced orange seller and pass on. First we see the blacks. Then whites. Fruitseller looks at the watch, then at the sun, and quickly follows the crowd—some of who are greatly amused by 'his' salesman's antics.

FRUITSELLER: Utamu . . . Gacamirwo-oo
Ukimeza, chozi lajimwaga!
Ni utamuuu . . . tam-tamuuuuu . . .
Kuheherwona gucamirwo.
[*The cries fade away.*]

Court

*Scene changes to inside the court. Note that the stage should
be such that the street can easily be changed into a courtroom.
Whites enter, women dressed as if for a show, fanning their
faces. Men swagger in with pistols belted around their waists.
They sit on one side of the court. As the Africans enter, it should
be a study in contrast with their torn clothes and tattered shoes.
They are frisked by the African soldiers under Waitina's orders.
Sticks or anything that might suggest a weapon are removed
from them. N.B. Throughout the court scenes, Africans are
defiant towards the settlers and the colonial authorities while
appreciative of Kimathi's stand. The court clerk is busy looking
at some files, scribbling something, and putting a few things
on the Judge's bench.*
*In the court, blacks and whites sit on separate sides. It is as if
a huge gulf lies between them. The air is still and tense. To
break the tension, people on both sides try to make conversation
in low voices. The clerk orders them to keep quiet—meaning
the blacks more than the whites, but really to no people in
particular. One of the settlers walks to the clerk and holds him
up by the collar.*

SETTLER: How dare you?
CLERK: I'm sorry, sir, I'm sorry sir!

*Africans hiss and some make as if to move forward. A few whites
take out their guns.*

23

CLERK: I was telling them, sir . . . not you. God above, not you.

A white police officer comes forward in a hurry.

POLICE OFFICER: Hold back your guns! And get back to your seats.

The aggressive settler and whites with guns put up some resistance mumbling and complaining about the cheek of "educated black chaps". Eventually they sit back, resentfully. The clerk tries to adjust his collar, coughs, and sits down. Suddenly, he jumps up.

CLERK: Court, rise.

Enter Shaw Henderson dressed as a judge. Not in disguise. He should in fact be seen to believe in his role as a judge, to acquire the grave airs of a judge. Judge sits down. The audience sit. Clerk gives him the file. Judge looks at it.

JUDGE: Call the prisoner.

Hushed silence. Judge tries to look unconcerned, dignified, but he too ends up staring in the same direction as the others. Clink. Clink . . . Dedan Kimathi is brought in under heavy guard, with chains on his feet and chains on his hands. He is pushed into the witness box by Waitina who is flanked by First and Second soldiers.
Dead silence

JUDGE: Dedan Kimathi s/o Wachiuri, alias Prime Minister, or Field Marshal, of no fixed address, you are charged that on the night of Sunday, October the 21st, 1956, at or near Ihururu in Nyeri District, you were found in possession of a firearm, namely a revolver, without a licence, contrary to section 89 of the penal code, which under Special Emergency Regulations constitutes a criminal offence. Guilty or not guilty?
[*Dedan Kimathi remains silent.*]

I may warn you that your silence could be construed as contempt of court in which case I could order that you be sent for a certain term in jail.

[*Kimathi remains silent; there is murmuring in court. Judge hammers on the bench.*]

Silence in court. I will repeat the charge: Dedan Kimathi s/o Wachiuri, you are charged that on the night of Sunday, October the 21st, 1956, at or near Ihururu in Nyeri District, you were found in possession of a firearm, namely a revolver, without a licence, contrary to section 89 of the penal code, which under Special Emergency Regulations constitutes a criminal offence. Guilty or not guilty?

KIMATHI: By what right dare you, a colonial judge, sit in judgement over me?

JUDGE: [*playing with his glasses, oozing infinite patience*]: Kimathi, I may remind you that we are in a court of law.

KIMATHI: An imperialist court of law.

JUDGE: I may remind you that you are charged with a most serious crime. It carries a death sentence.

KIMATHI: Death. . . .

JUDGE: Yes, death. . . .

KIMATHI: To a criminal judge, in a criminal court, set up by criminal law: the law of oppression. I have no words.

JUDGE: Perhaps you don't understand. Myabe your long stay in the Forest has . . . I mean . . . we are here to deal fairly with you, to see that justice is done. Even handed justice.

KIMATHI: I will not plead to a law in which we had no part in the making.

JUDGE: Law is law. The rule of law is the basis of every civilized community. Justice is justice.

KIMATHI: Whose law? Whose justice?

JUDGE: There is only one law, one justice.

KIMATHI: Two laws. Two justices. One law and one justice protects the man of property, the man of wealth, the foreign exploiter.

25

Another law, another justice, silences the poor, the hungry, our people.

[*Jubilance and excitement among the Africans. Fury in the faces of settlers. Tension.*]

JUDGE: I am not talking about the laws of Nyandarua jungle.

KIMATHI: The jungle of colonialism? Of exploitation? For it is there that you'll find creatures of prey feeding on the blood and bodies of those who toil: those who make the earth yield. Us.
Those who make factories roar
Those who wait and groan for a better day tomorrow
The maimed
Their backs bent
Sweat dripping down their shoulders
Beaten
Starved
Despised
Spat on
Whipped
But refusing to be broken
Waiting for a new dawn
Dawn on Mount Kenya.

JUDGE: I know you are a poet, an orator, a politician. No society can be without laws to protect property . . . I mean protect our lives . . . Civilisation . . . Investment . . . Christianity . . . Order. [*the aggressive settler sits back pronouncing through a loud whisper*: "*Damn right*" *other settlers murmur approvingly. The judge says nothing.*]

KIMATHI: I despise your laws and your courts. What have they done for our people? What?
Protected the oppressor. Licensed the murderers of the people: Our people,
whipped when they did not pick your tea leaves

your coffee beans
Imprisoned when they refused to "ayah"
your babies
and "boy" your houses and gardens
Murdered when they didn't rickshaw
your ladies and your gentlemen.
I recognize only one law, one court:
the court and the law of those who
fight against exploitation,
The toilers armed to say
We demand our freedom.
That's the eternal law of the oppressed,
of the humiliated, of the injured, the insulted!
Fight
Struggle
Change.

JUDGE: There's no liberty without law and order.

KIMATHI: There is no order and law without
liberty.
Chain my legs,
Chain my hands,
Chain my soul,
And you cry, law and justice?
And the law of the people bids me:
Unchain my hands
Unchain my legs
Unchain my soul!

Some blacks clap. Whites hiss. Guards stand on the alert.

JUDGE: Order in court! [*he rises*]: Court adjourned. Prisoner re-
manded in custody until tomorrow when the court resumes.

*Court rises. The judge walks out. The minute his cloak dis-
appears behind the door, the aggressive settler walks towards
the prisoner, swearing hysterically. The other settlers look*

ready to strike. The guards get hold of Kimathi and begin to move out hastily.

SETTLER: [*pointing his gun at Kimathi as he is whisked out of the court and screaming at the top of his voice*]: Bloody bastard Mau Mau. And the cheek! British justice has gone beyond limits to tolerate this, this kind of rudeness from a mad, bushwog. [*shouting frantically to the already departed guards*]: Hold it askari or I'll shoot you together with that bush communist. [*shouting even louder while the audience in court gaze at him in terror*]: Field Marshall/Prime Minister. Fucking black monkey. Listen, you'll die now, wog. I'll teach you justice. [*makes for the open door through which the guarded Kimathi has just left. Then abruptly, hysterically, he turns back and faces the tense court audience*]:

I had cattle and sheep—by the thousands:
Where are they now?
I had acres of maize and wheat:
Where are they now?
I had a wife and daughter:
Where are they now?
Killed. Burnt. Maimed
by this lunatic and his pack of bandits.
Which innocent investor can sleep these days?
Beer and whisky are stale and bitter.
Look at me. I am no idler.
I may not be a Delamere or a Grogan
But I am a worker
I came to this country as a soldier
A simple soldier.
Fighting against banks, mortgages,
the colonial office, the whole lot
on my back.

[*Pointing the gun to the African side of the audience. Anger and defiance greet him*]:

You think it was easy?
And when I thought I would
sit down and enjoy the fruits of my labour
You struck.
I had perfect relationships with my boys
They were happy on my farm
I gave them posho, built them a school,
a dispensary . . . gave them everything
they needed
They loved me
Yes, at Olkalau they talked of
my farm with awe: loyal, meek, submissive.
Then that devil, Field Marshal, came
Milk clerk, oath clerk, murderer!
Poisoned simple minds
led astray their God-fearing souls
with his black mumbo jumbo
My wife, my daughter, my property.
Now, now, you'll die.

[*Screaming and chaos as the settler threatens to shoot. He holds the ground in such a way that the only means of escape would have to be through the windows.*]

OLD WHITE DAME: Stop it, Dick! [*really frantically.*] Someone, take the gun from him quickly. It's all the doing of these wild savages. [*Hostile reaction from some of the Africans.*]

WHITE OFFICER: [*walks in with several African KAR soldiers. Addressing himself to the white settler*]: Mr. Windhoek, put away the gun. The law will see justice done.

SETTLER: [*resisting and thundering away*]:
The law my foot! Did you hear that crank?
Did you hear the cheek?
And the blasted judge listened to it all.
No! No! This gun will be the judge!
[*struggling with the white officer, foaming with rage like a madman*]: Field Marshal, Sir Ded . . . Ded . . . Kimathi.

29

You will die at my hand. [*As the officer struggles with Windhoek, the gun explodes. The officer overpowers him and takes him out. The court disperses amid unresolved controversy as soldiers clear out the people.*]

Street

FRUITSELLER (WOMAN): Oranges cheap today
Oranges cheap today
Thandaraita-i
Kuheherwo na gucamirwo
Thandaraita-aaaaaaa!
[*Fruitseller mixes with people coming out of the court. They ignore him, but he goes on singing his wares. People go and the fruitseller is left alone on the stage. He looks about as if seeking out somebody*]:
Thandaraita-i
Thandaraita-aaaaaaa!
Kuheherwo
Kuheherwo na gucamirwo
Tamu-uuuuuu!
Ukimeza chozi lajimwaga
Thandaraita-i
Thandaraita-aaaaaaaa
On your way to heaven
You gonna get an orange.

Goes out. Enter Boy. Holding the loaf of bread.

BOY: She told me that he would be around here. But I have not seen an orange seller or any fruitseller. What a woman! Why would she not take the bread herself? Afraid. That's it. Afraid. Why should she expect me to risk my life taking bread, just a loaf of bread to Kimathi? In any case, they say that Kimathi does not eat bread. And suppose it's not Kimathi, and it is his double, his shadow whom they have arrested? [*makes as if to move*]: But where shall I find her? Where can I get her? I know. She did not want me to take the loaf to anybody. She wanted to test me. To see if I would eat the bread. [*breaks a piece*]: But she said she would be watching me all the time. [*he tries to return the piece patching up the loaf. He is so absorbed in this exercise that he does not see the girl enter. She sees him. Hesitates. Tries to walk across stealthily. He sees her. Forgets about the broken piece.*]

BOY: Hey. You. My money!

GIRL: I've no money.

BOY: I'll show you.

[*he tries to block the girl's path but she slips past the boy and she runs off the stage. The boy picks up the loaf of bread and runs after the girl.*]

First Trial

All four trials of Dedan Kimathi take place in his cell. But the cell should remind us of the courtroom and should be bare and harsh. Kimathi sits in a corner, long chain from his leg dragging behind him. He is also heavily guarded. When Henderson enters, Kimathi is leaning against the wall. He glides into the cell, checking his movement at the entrance to listen to Kimathi as he is talking to himself.

KIMATHI: Dreams. Visions.
Karuna-ini
Ihururu
Muthunduri
Sugarcane valleys of my youth
Green ridges of my childhood.
Ndi-ini stream
Where I used to bathe
Plunging naked into the cool waters!
They visit me now

These places and forest paths
of my beginnings.
[*He now addresses an invisible presence—a mental silhouette of his crazed mother.*]
Poor mother . . . No . . . don't cry.
I was right to choose the path of struggle.
How else would I have looked you in the eyes?
Forgive me Forgive me.
That your love for me
Has turned your head
To wild imaginings!
Victory will be ours
Mother of us, your children.

HENDERSON: Hey, Dedan. Field Marshal. Guilty visitation?

KIMATHI: Who are you?

HENDERSON: Bwana Shaw Henderson. All your people know me. I'm a friend.

KIMATHI: Shaw Henderson! Friend and killer of Africans, ugh!

HENDERSON: The trouble with you, Dedan, is that you are too suspicious. Look, I come peacefully. I'm not armed.

KIMATHI: [*severely*]: No, not with a firearm. Only with words. Speeches. Sweet promises. Save your breath.

HENDERSON: Look here, Dedan. Your people trust me. They have sent me to talk sense into your obstinate head.

KIMATHI: You lie! Which people? Loyalists? Homeguards? Traitors! Simpletons! These are your people. [*Chuckles sarcastically, bitterly*]: Lenana, Wang'ombe, Karuri Gakure, Njiri, Waruhiu, Luka Kinyanjui, Mumia . . . Look, Shaw Henderson—friend of the Africans—you cannot deceive me even in your many disguises. Just as you came in I had seen you in my dreams. All the slaves you have deceived in the past. Raider of slaves!

HENDERSON: Your dreams again? Do you remember the letter you once wrote your brother Wambararia?

KIMATHI: Why tire my ears with names of traitors?

HENDERSON: You never liked him, did you? He too is helping us.

KIMATHI: He sold out for his stomach.

HENDERSON: You feared his rivalry . . . for leadership? You feared everybody's rivalry. General China. Stanley Mathenge.

KIMATHI: Rivalry? I have never feared anybody's rivalry. I have only sought to protect the struggle from betrayal, opportunism and regional chauvinism.

HENDERSON: [in an effort to flatter]: That's why you must live.

KIMATHI: What do you mean live? British Imperialist arrogance! Who are you to grant or deny life?

HENDERSON: Listen, Kimathi. I come to make a deal.

KIMATHI: Deals! Pacts! Treaties! How many nations have you wiped out, and later said: well, according to this treaty and that treaty, they had ceded their land and their lives.

HENDERSON: Look here, Dedan. I'm a plain soldier. It's true that at times I play the Special Branch, a hunter of men, but at heart I'm a soldier. "To the point" is a soldier's motto. You see, I am not a poet and a dreamer like you. You must plead in court tomorrow. And you must plead guilty.

KIMATHI: Plead? Guilty? Pleading guilty? Guilty pleading.

HENDERSON: Now, now, don't lash at me with those red eyes.

KIMATHI: Do you think you deceived me?

HENDERSON: When?

KIMATHI: Today. In your court of jesters.

HENDERSON: What do you mean?

KIMATHI: I must say you looked rather splendid in your prosecuting Judge's robes. Even handed justice.

HENDERSON: I'm serious in my offer.

KIMATHI: Go on. What's your offer? The next trick?

HENDERSON: I've told you, you are too suspicious. It's not a trick. I give you my word as a British Gentleman. Plead guilty. We spare you life.

KIMATHI: You? Spare my life? What's at the root of this imperial magnanimity? I thought there was a prize on my head.

HENDERSON: I'm a soldier. I called it a deal, not magnanimity. We want this war to end. Stanley Mathenge is still at large. Your confession and your co-operation would bring them all out.

KIMATHI: And you would get another George Medal! Medals! Medals! Must you kill people, wipe out nations for medals?

HENDERSON: Look, between the two of us, we don't need to pretend. Nations live by strength and self-interest. You challenged our interests: we had to defend them. It is to our mutual interest and for your own good that we should end this ugly war.

KIMATHI: Wiles. Luring voices of poisonous serpents. Do you take me for a fool?

HENDERSON: It was the same with all the others. China. Gati. Hungu. Gaceru. And even Wambararia, your own brother! All our collaborators. At first they would not believe that I meant every word I said. But look, we have spared their lives.

KIMATHI: H'm. You mean you took prisoner their lives!

HENDERSON: Why must you twist what I say like that, Dedan? Look, you may not believe this either, but you are very special to me. Don't you remember how we used to play together as children, on the slopes of Mount Kenya? Remember the day we played Horse and Rider? We fell. [he laughs.]

KIMATHI: You mean I threw you off! And you went sniffing and crying to your mother.

HENDERSON: You must admit you were rather nasty!

KIMATHI: Yes. You wanted me to play the horse. And you the rider.

HENDERSON: Well, my friend, there has to be a horse and a rider. What would be the point of the game?

KIMATHI: There must be horses and riders, must there? Well, let me be Balaam's ass then. [chuckles]: Yes, the one who rejected his rider. [pause]: When the hunted has truly learnt to hunt his hunter, then the hunting game will be no more.

HENDERSON: You don't keep your mind out of the forest for long, do you? What is the good of these blood-baths? Your people are the losers, Dedan.

KIMATHI: With the British, we have been losers all the way—yes— but this is a new era. This is a new war. We have bled for you. We have fought your wars for you, against the Germans, Japanese, Italians. This time we shall bleed for our soil, for our freedom, until you let go.

34

HENDERSON: You are dreaming again.

KIMATHI: Yes. And I will keep on dreaming till my visions come true and our people are free.

HENDERSON: [*frustrated in his efforts to make Kimathi cave in. There's a note of desperation in his flattery and sudden inward-lookingness*]: I'll be frank with you, Dedan. I admire your courage. Your pride. I love your country and your people. That is the only reason why I come as a friend to try and pers—

KIMATHI: [*shouting impatiently*]: Kimathi wa Wachiuri will never betray the people's liberation struggle. Never!

HENDERSON: Look. Listen to me for your own good. [*Kimathi obstinately turns away, but Henderson proceeds with his monologue*]: I know all about colonization. My father came from Scotland. . . . We too have been ruled by the English. Again I'll be frank with you, Emperor Jones. It's true that in Scotland he would not have had it so good. There fortune was the Lochness Monster that many dream of but only a few can see. Here it was good. Loans. Clubs. Gymkhana. The Royal Hunt, Limuru Hunt, the envy of aristocrats. By the way, that speech of yours in court was nice. You were right. But as a Judge I was supposed to be neutral. Struggle. We too have a right to struggle, to persevere, conserve, maintain healthy standards: Christianity, civilization. I am a Kenyan. By might and right. Right is might, believe me. I grew up in Nyeri. I'm only fighting for my own, spoils of war if you like. But sweat and thought have gone into it. Dedan Kimathi: you must plead. Life comes before pride. You once vowed that no whiteman would ever get you. But now you are in custody. Hanging between life and death. Plead, plead, plead guilty. It's a game, yes. You can name your prize. You'll have your life. Only, we must end this strife. Plead guilty for Life!

KIMATHI: [*angry, grabs him by the neck*]:
Life. My Life. Give up my life for your life.
Who are you, imperialist cannibal, to guarantee my life?
My life is our People
Struggling

Fighting
Not like you to maintain
Slavery
Oppression
Exploitation
But
To end slavery, exploitation,
Modern cannibalism. Out. Rat.
Go back to your masters
and tell them:
Kimathi will never sell Kenya
to the British or to any other
Breed of man-eaters, now or in the years to come.

HENDERSON: Warder! Warder!
[*doors open. Warders rush in with guns drawn.*
Kimathi lets him go.]

HENDERSON: [*panting*.]: I'll get you yet. I swear I'll get you. I, Shaw
Henderson, will break you. I know the native mind. Black
man, I'll have the last laugh. [*goes out.*]

Second Trial

KIMATHI: Save your life. A colonialist my saviour?
Saved into neo-slavery. Listen to that my people!
Kimathi of Iregi generation.
I was blessed by a blind grandmother,
A peasant, a toiler.
She imparted her strength, the strength
of our people into me.
I felt her blind faith, blind strength
enter my bones. Fire and light.
Save my life?
Maybe that and this and that!
It is true that I've always wanted
to dance the dance of my people.

MIME: [*Group of dancers, performing a sequence of dances by different peoples of Kenya take up the arena in turns. Each group dances its part and then walks right across the stage and stands aside.*]

KIMATHI: They used to dance these
Before the white colonialist came
In the arena . . . at initiation . . .
during funerals . . . during marriage . . .
Then the colonialist came
And the people danced
a different dance.

A colonial governor arrives. The dance now by all the groups together becomes one of fear and humiliation. They dance feverishly and then go off the stage followed by the stiff figure of the colonial governor.

KIMATHI: Oh, my people!
How can we sing and dance like this
In a strange land?
How can we sing and dance like this
When water everywhere is bitter?
How can we dance the dance of humiliation and fear?
These were . . . no, *are* the questions.
To wrestle with them,
I became an organizer of youth,
We collected from the seven ridges around Karunaini.
Gichamu we called ourselves
And we devised new dances
Talking of the struggle before us
Readying ourselves for the war.

MIME: [*The dancers return, singing a song of struggle and performing a militant dance.*]

KIMATHI: We stood on Githuri hill
To our left, Nyandarua Forest ridge

To our right, Mount Kenya
And between them
Below our eyes
Stretching to beyond Nanyuki and Naro Moru
Nyeri plains and lands stolen from us.
We asked ourselves
How long shall we
Gichamu Karunaini youth
of Iregi Generation
Allow our people to continue
Slaves of hunger, disease, sorrow
In our own lands
While foreigners eat
And snore in bed with fullness?

Enter a Banker's delegation—or a Trade-cum-businessman's delegation. The white man in the delegation should, in dress and manner, epitomise the money-owning class of imperialist Europe. The other one is Indian. A third is an African who does not speak at all, but keeps on nodding his head in agreement.

BANKER: You are right Dedan. Hunger. Disease. Ignorance. Those are the true enemies of your people.

KIMATHI: Who are you?

BANKER: Time is money. I am, or rather, we are from the Banks, the Insurance companies, the industries. You can call us . . . the representatives of the business community. You see, Dedan, this war is holding back investment, the flow of money, development.

KIMATHI: Development! Money. Is money development?

BANKER: I don't blame you. You may be a little deficient on the side of . . . eh, economics, and history. I was here before you were born. Standard Bank. National and Grindlays Bank. Barclays. I am the maker of modern Kenya. Who financed the railways?

MIME: [*Coolies and Swahilis building the Railway. They are driven away by Nandi warriors led by Koitalel.*]

BANKER: You see. Your people again. Their ten-year-armed resistance only ruined the chances of progress. But when the job was finished see now the dividends: Settlers. Delamere. Hunters. Soldiers of fortune. We were behind them all. Now, you'll agree with me that they did transform this land. Mombasa, Nairobi, Nakuru, Eldoret, Kitale, Kisumu. Modern cities. Modern Highways.

KIMATHI: Come clean. What do you want? I was not fighting the Banks.

BANKER: Ha! ha! ha! You are a wise man, Dedan. Yes, there's no need to fight the Banks. We are your true friends. At first we were a little apprehensive about a blackman's government. . . . We thought that it might, well, be a danger to investment, assets, and all that . . . But . . . we have since learnt one or two truths from Ghana, Nigeria, Liberia and even India.

INDIAN: True! True! Dedan. In India—a, ve got our independent. Preedom. To make money. This here, our true priend. Not racialism. Leaves your custom alone. You can pray Budha, pray Confucius, pray under the trees, pray rocks, vear sari . . . your culture . . . songs . . . dances . . . ve don't mind . . . propided . . . ve make money . . . priend . . . priend.

KIMATHI: [*excited*]: Some of our people passed through India on their way from Burma. Calcutta. Delhi. Bombay. They told of hungry peoples, beggars on pavements . . . wives selling themselves for a rupee . . . . Have they now said "no" to poverty?

INDIAN: Ve trying. Little. Little. But ve hawe our religion. Ve hawe our plag. Ve hawe national anthem. And now ewen Indian Bankers. Ha! ha!

BANKER: Listen. We are now prepared to settle for a black man's government. In patnership. Only. . . .

KIMATHI: Only?

BANKER: Confess. Repent. Plead guilty. Co-operate—like the surrendered generals. Tell your people to come out of the Forest. We need stability. There never can be progress without stability. Then we can finance big Hotels . . . International Hotels . . . Seaside resorts . . . Night Clubs . . . Casinos . . . Tarmac roads . . . oil refineries and pipelines . . . Then tourists from USA, Germany, France, Switzerland, Japan, will flock in. Investment, my friend, development, prosperity, happiness.

KIMATHI: And my people?

BANKER: Who are your people?

KIMATHI: The oppressed of the land . . . all those whose labour power has transformed this land. For it is not true that it was your money that built this country. It was our sweat. It was our hands. Where do our people come in in your partnership for progress?

BANKER: Toilers there will always be. Even in America, England, France, Germany, Switzerland, Sweden, Japan . . . all the civilized world. There are servants and masters . . . sellers of labour and buyers of labour. Masters and servants.

INDIAN: True! True! Ewen in holy religion . . . there are vorkers . . . Brahmins and untouchables.

KIMATHI: The religion of enslavement! Like colonialism which makes the colonized sweat and bleed while master comes to harvest.

BANKER: Racialism . . . No. Colour Bar . . . No. This may have been necessary in the 1930s. But now with more and more educated black people [*points at the African who nods*] there's obviously no need for colour discrimination. We have grown wiser.

INDIAN: True! True!

KIMATHI: Money . . . for a sell-out of our people . . . NEVER.

BANKER: As I said: Time is money. Think about it.

KIMATHI: [*specifically pointing at the African businessman*] Judas!

They go out.

40

Street

Enter Girl, walking slowly, meditatively.

GIRL: I'm . . . tired . . . of . . . running. All my life I have been running. On the run. On the road. Men molesting me. I was once a dutiful daughter. A nice Christian home. It was in the settled area. CHRIST IS THE HEAD OF THIS HOUSE THE UNSEEN GUEST AT EVERY MEAL THE SILENT LISTENER TO EVERY CONVERSATION. I ran away from school because the headmaster wanted to do wicked things with me. Always: you remain behind. You take the wood to my house. You take this chalk and books to the office. Then he would follow me and all he wanted was to touch my breasts. So, I left school. I wanted to stay home and teach myself how to sew or do something with my life. But my father would have nothing of it. He called me an idler and sent me to pick tea leaves for that cruel settler, Mr. Jones. How he used to abuse and punish us! I had to run away from home, from my father, from Mr. Jones . . . . In the city it was the boys. Always harassing me . . . And yet I did not want to starve! I lost my virginity while trying to run away from losing it. How else could I live?

Yet, the money was so miserable. And sometimes they would beat me afterwards, calling me a child. No. I'll not run away again. A girl cannot run, run, run all her life.

Enter Boy.

BOY: [*not noticing the girl*]: I feel so ashamed. I forgot the woman's words: she said I should never beat the girl again. And now I feel as though she is watching me, admonishing me. I feel so ashamed.

VOICE: Just now you are a beast and the girl was right to call you a brute.

Girl takes out a knife, from underneath her skirt. Boy sees her. But he is genuinely sorry.

41

BOY: I don'ι want to fight with you.

GIRL: [*venom in her voice*]: Coward.

BOY: I really mean it.

GIRL: Coward.

BOY: I want to apologize.

GIRL: A trick. Coward. Bully. Brute. I'll not run away from you. I'll never run away from anybody. Never.

They stare at one another in silence, the Girl panting with anger, walking, knife in hand, towards him. They circle one another, as if weighing up one another.

BOY: Drop that thing.

GIRL: Come on, Brute Boy, Bully Boy.

BOY: Drop that thing I tell you. Do you know what I am going to do with you? Get hold of you. Put you on my lap. Slap, slap your buttocks. Just to show you that I don't want to play with you. I don't want the money back. You can keep it. You needed it as much as I did. I was foolish to fight you over it. But unless you drop that thing. . . .

GIRL: [*holding herself by the hips and jetting out saliva in challenge*]: All cowards, all brutes and bullies behave the same way. Show fear, a tail in your mouth, and they threaten thunder and rain. They humiliate you, insult you, injure you. Show that you are a human being: struggle, fight back and it becomes their turn to run away, to flatter you, to try and make you their friends. Bully Boy: let's see your manhood; or are you scared of a girl?

Boy stung by this now puts away the bread and walks determinedly towards her. But her knife is ready. They circle one another, both breathing hard, watching each other's movement. Suddenly, he grips her hand; the hand holding the knife. They wrestle. He manages to twist her hand. Knife falls. He kicks it toward where the loaf of bread is. They continue wrestling. He can lift her off the ground but he cannot fell her. Suddenly they both fall to the ground. They roll struggling toward where the

knife and the bread are. Boy gets to the knife; throws it away.
Girl rolls him over. She gets the Bread and throws it, smashing
it on the floor. Gun falls out of the loaf. Both see it. They are
suddenly frozen into each other. She is scared. He too is scared.
He stands up and takes the gun. Examines it with trembling hands.

BOY: [*bitterly*]: The woman. Orange seller. Dedan Kimathi. Lies. Lies. I now see it all.

GIRL: What is it?

BOY: She wanted to get rid of it and land me in trouble, in jail. Again.

GIRL: What . . . what's it all about?

BOY: Listen. You must help me. We must help one another. What shall I do with it?

GIRL: But how did you get it?

BOY: It was that woman. I'll report it to the police. I don't want to die!

GIRL: If you report it, they'll surely kill you, call you a terrorist.

BOY: The cursed woman.

VOICE: The day you'll understand why your father died: the day you'll ask yourself whether it was right for him to die so; the day you'll ask yourself—what can I do so that another shall not be made to die under such grisly circumstances, that day, my son, you'll become a man. [*Boy is mesmerized as if in a trance.*]

GIRL: What's it?

BOY: Didn't you hear her?

GIRL: Who?

BOY: The woman.

GIRL: When? Where? Why do you tremble so?
   [*She asks that resting her hand on his shoulder.*]

BOY: No, no, not now, Mama.
   But how can I turn
   Against her call
   And
   Live?

43

Third Trial

KIMATHI: [*groaning. Turning from side to side*]: I knew it; the invisible powers behind them all. So smooth, so confident, heartless, soulless. Banker . . . Industrialist . . . Settler . . . Governor . . . Police . . . Army . . . Judge . . . all one. Drinkers of Darkness. Drinkers of blood. Ha! Ha! Why should I fear? Our people will see through the smiles, through this sudden avowal of friendship. And yet . . . suppose . . . if . . . if . . . save my life? No . . . Dreams . . . Temptations . . . People. [*shouts*]: Our people!

Enter an African Business Executive, dressed like an Englishman, politician, and a Priest. The Priest remains still in one spot.

BUSINESS EXECUTIVE: Yes, our people, your people, all our people. Black is beautiful. Black Power.

KIMATHI: I seem to know you. Who are you? I've been sitting on hot coals of trials and temptations. Ease my heart, my brothers. In this infernal corner, this narrow wretched corner, chained to the walls, chained to the floor . . . Why, one almost loses one's head.

BUSINESS EXECUTIVE: You know me. You know me. I have stood by you. Wa Wachiuri, it has been a long struggle. I've given money to the cause. My shop at Masira was an oathing centre.

KIMATHI: I think I know of you. And many like you. We have travelled thus far, this road together. Thank you. A few of us fell by the wayside. They were deceived by the enemy and became his homeguards. Spear bearers. But in the main, we have held together. Thank you for your, aah, cheque-book contribution to the struggle. Hereafter we will teach solidarity to a divided world.

BUSINESS EXECUTIVE: [*coughs*]: That's why I, we, have come. I have not much time. I wanted to ask you: don't you think we have won the war?

KIMATHI: How you still my soul with your words! We shall win the war. For, let me tell the fainthearted that this our struggle will continue until we seize back the right and the ability to make ourselves new men and women in our own land.

BUSINESS EXECUTIVE: We have already won.

KIMATHI: In spirit, yes. The spirit of our people, their will to life, freedom and power . . . this will never be broken. Your words of confidence and faith in our ultimate victory makes these chains light as feathers. For more of such words, I can take more, more . . . .

BUSINESS EXECUTIVE: [*impatiently*]: Listen, Dedan. We have won the war.

KIMATHI: [*struck by the words*]: What? Have our oppressors surrendered? Freedom. We shall drive them out of our land, this earth, my brothers. Put our house in order. Build anew. Oh, the years of pain! And you spear-bearers, where will you run to when the braves return under deafening sounds of drums proclaiming victory? But have they? My friends, you are twice welcome for bringing such news. My heart is full like Gura River in flood. Have they really? So long, so soon? Break these chains. Unchain my heart, my soul! Unchain four centuries of chains. Kenya, our dearly bought, fought for motherland.

BUSINESS EXECUTIVE: It is not, eeh, exactly like that. But there have been two important announcements. They have said: No more racialism. No more colour bar. In public places. In administration. In business. In the allocation of loans. In the grabbing, well, in the acquisition of land. Partnership in progress, that's the new motto. Is this not what we have been fighting for? Any black man who now works hard and has capital can make it to the top. We can become local directors of foreign companies. We can now buy land in the White Highlands. White Highlands no more. It's now: willing Seller, willing Buyer.

KIMATHI: What new song is this? Buy back our land from those who stole it from us? Our land? Have we not bought it with streams of blood? Rivers of sweat?

BUSINESS EXECUTIVE: No free things. Colour bar is out. Banks are open to all. What more do *we* want?

KIMATHI: And politics? Independence? Is this too for sale?

POLITICIAN: We have been given two alternatives. We can get independence, province by province. Majimboism. As a token of their goodwill, they have now allowed District and Provincial Political Parties. Independence for Central Province. After all, it's we Gikuyu, Embu and Meru who really fought for Uhuru.

KIMATHI: Would you too call the war for national liberation a regional Movement? What has colonialism done to your thinking? [*Pause. Firmly but coolly*]: Hear me. Kenya is one indivisible whole. The cause we fight for is larger than provinces; it shatters ethnic barriers. It is a whole people's cause.

POLITICIAN: There! You speak as if you can read my mind. The second alternative before us, you see, is to receive uhuru as one people.

KIMATHI: Receive uhuru! And since when did our people become beggars? Who are you? How can you decide for the people? Have they released our people from concentration camps? Have they released Jomo Kenyatto? Paul Ngei? Fred Kubai? Where is Achieng Oneko? Bildad Kaggia? Kungu Karumba? Are they out? Tell me more!

POLITICIAN: They will be out soon. Personally, nothing concerns me more than their release. Everyone is fighting for their freedom. Tom Mboya, Ronald Ngala, Oginga Odinga, Daniel Moi, Julius Kiano. Petitions all over the country. Marches. Posters. Oh, let them come out. Then we shall form one country-wide political party and serious negotiations will soon be in progress. In State House. In London. We shall sit around a conference table. We shall be given independence.

KIMATHI: Give! Given! Give! Given! Given! Beggars. Hands outstretched. Ten cents. Thirty pieces of silver. Independence on a silver platter? Away. Vile creatures. Rats. Blood suckers. What? Blood? Yes. Your people's blood. Our people's blood. The blood of us workers and peasants. Yes, those are our people. And you, New Farmers, New Settlers: Black skins, colonial settlers' hearts. Thousands of acres of wheat, tea, coffee, pyrethrum . . . ranches . . . while workers and peasants

live in hovels, landless in villages! New African Bankers
... I now understand ... loans ... token shares in banks,
companies ... Grab shops ... Grab gems, Transport Buses,
land ... Grab, Grab, Grab.

Partnership in Progress. Towards what end? What will you do
to the widows, orphans, the labouring millions? New masters.
We labour for you, pick coffee and tea for you. Is that why
poor men died and continue to die in the forests? General
Kago, Baimunge, Matenjagwo ... and many brave sons are
still locked in there ... Stanley Mathenge ....

Have you been there to see them, hear them, planning, talking,
dreaming, fighting for a new world, a human world? We have
won. We have won. What's the prize, new drinkers of honey
from human skulls?

POLITICIAN: We all fought for Uhuru in our different way. I think
it unwise ... a little hasty ... divisive politics to single out
certain people, certain classes as having fought for Uhuru.
There are no classes in Africa. We are all freedom
fighters.

KIMATHI: The prize. I asked, the prize. Slaves. What's the prize for
our second slavery?

BUSINESS EXECUTIVE: We call it off.

KIMATHI: Call. Uncall. What?

POLITICIAN: War in the Forest. Words will now do. They have
already given us seats in the Legislative Council. Great victory.

KIMATHI: Words. Words. Words. Game of diplomats!

BUSINESS EXECUTIVE: Plead guilty. Save your life. Save lives. Join us.

KIMATHI: Cursed minds! What revolution will unchain these minds!
Out. Out. Neo-slaves.

[business Executive and Politician go out]:

And you, man of the collar? Collared man?

Accompany them to the plantations. New overseers of our
slaughter.

PRIEST: [coming out of the shadows]: My calling is a little different.
Things of the world. Why, in my father's house are many
mansions.

47

KIMATHI: Even you my father . . . Tell me, tell me, do you think . . . no but it is not possible . . . can you look beyond these walls. . . . Are our people still fighting? Or have they given up like those two fools who have joined forces with the enemy?

PRIEST: I've told you. My kingdom is not of this world.

KIMATHI: Don't rouse my anger against your holy beard. What do you mean?

PRIEST: The world passeth away and the lust thereof, but the word of God abideth for ever. I know you love the Bible. You always read a few verses from the holy book. . . . [*Priest reads as if he is Kimathi in the Forest. He holds an invisible Bible firmly in both hands*]:

Lamentations, Chapter 5, verses 1 to 9.

"Remember, O Lord, what is come upon us: consider and behold our reproach.

Our inheritance is turned to strangers, our houses to aliens.

We are orphans and fatherless, our mothers are as widows.

We have drunken our water for money; our wood is sold unto us.

Our necks are under persecution: we labour, and have no rest.

We have given the land to the Egyptians, and to the Assyrians, to be satisfied with bread.

Our fathers have sinned, and are not; and we have borne their iniquities.

Servants have ruled over us: there is none that doth deliver us out of their hand.

We get our bread with the peril of our lives because of the sword of the wilderness."

KIMATHI: [*continues by quoting from Ecclesiastes Chapter 4, Verse 1*]: "So I returned, and considered all the oppressions that are done under the sun: and behold the tears of such as were oppressed, and they had no comforter; and on the side of their oppressors there was power; but they had no comforter". Why? How did you—

PRIEST: Your Bible.

KIMATHI: I only read those sections necessary to our struggle.

PRIEST: You see, Dedan. That's where you went wrong. These verses are not talking about earthly things, earthly struggle. It is a spiritual struggle. God and Satan locked in an immortal struggle for the domination of our souls.

KIMATHI: And you? Policeman of the gospel? Warder of souls? How long will you continue being their messenger?

PRIEST: Wrong again. We are now Africanizing the Church. We want to see Christ reflected in our culture. Drums in Church. African Bishops. African Moderators. African Cardinals.

KIMATHI: Slave! Slave! when will you throw off your ill-fitting borrowed gown and create something you can truly call your own? Pastor, tell me the difference between padre and settler. Go on.

PRIEST: [excited]: Why? Why? You once saw the light. Admit, Dedan. You were once baptized.

KIMATHI: Out with Dedan. I am Kimathi wa Wachiuri . . . of Iregi Generation. No. Not your kind of light. In the forest I used to walk alone, meditations on the mountain tops. I have walked all the lengths of the land between Kirinyaga and Nyandarua.

PRIEST: You were always a lonely, suspicious man. But then, some of your witchdoctors betrayed you. Jesus will never betray you.

KIMATHI: Betrayal. Betrayal. Prophets. Seers. Strange. I have always been suspicious of those who would preach cold peace in the face of violence. Turn the other cheek. Don't struggle against those that clothe themselves as butterflies. Collaborators.

PRIEST: Surrender your heart, Dedan. Let Jesus speak to you today.

KIMATHI: [continuing his speech as it were]: I have spoken with the God of my ancestors in dreams and on the mountain and not once did he counsel me to barter for my soul. One day, looking at the mountains, listening to the murmurings from Gura River, thinking about the braves of our people—those who have always resisted—I thought I saw a glimpse of Kenya to come: workers joining hands from the Coast to the Lake, making rivers, volcanoes, thunderbolts in the sky, making all these

powermonsters of nature administer to their needs and desires.
Man slave of Nature? Nature slave of man. Making no man
slave of any man. And voices welled up inside me. And I
felt the granite power of Kenyan people:
Let the volcanoes erupt fiery lava.
Uproot the trees.
Unchain the wind.
Open the doors of rain
Rivers, cataracts, rapids . . . Chain,
Chain these to your needs.
Deserts bloom
Harness yet Nature's energy and you shall
be the children of God—creators
of a new heaven on a new earth.

PRIEST: Don't blaspheme. You said you feared and fought the
seers?

KIMATHI: I feared the self-acclaimed messengers of God might
come to our fighters and say: surrender . . . that's the word of
God.

PRIEST: And don't you think it's time?

KIMATHI: You too!

PRIEST: Surrender. Call off bloodshed. New life, new Brotherhood
in Christ.

KIMATHI: And the blood *we* shed? Was that in vain?

PRIEST: We have all sinned and come short of the glory of God.
Why waste more lives? Plead guilty and ask God for forgive-
ness.

KIMATHI: Can it be wrong even in the eyes of your God for a people
to fight against exploitation? Cast out Lucifer. Tell me, old
man. Are people with whom we took the oath deserting us?

PRIEST: Think on my words, my child. There is wisdom in realism.
Enough is enough.

KIMATHI: This is what I always feared
How to discern our enemies
in black clothes, with sweet tongues,
Chequebook revolutionaries!

Go. Go. My trial has begun.
[*Priest does not move*]
I said Go! No, don't go. [*pause*]: Go.
Come to their jesters' court tomorrow.
Deserters! Yes. Come tomorrow.
You will hear my answer. Tomorrow. . . .
tomorrow. . . . I said Go!

Exit Priest.

Who are friends and who enemies?
Oh, the agony of a lone battle!
But I will fight on to the end
Alone. . . .
Alone, did I say?
No. Cast out these doubts!

Street

Same Day, late in the afternoon—almost verging onto evening light.
Boy and Girl. Can just see entrance to jailhouse. Warder stands at the entrance. Boy and Girl point at the jailhouse.

BOY: Look. There's a warder, moving up and down.
GIRL: Of course there's bound to be one. Did you expect them to leave all doors open without guards for all to walk right through? Go on. Let's speak to him.
WARDER: Get away. Where do you think you are going?
BOY: Please Mr. Warder, have you seen a man selling oranges around here?
WARDER: Around here so late in the evening? Who would buy them? Go away!

[*Boy and Girl move a few paces away.*]

BOY: I'm tired of it. I'm tired. We should throw it into a latrine or into the bush and forget the whole thing.

GIRL: Is that how to become a man? Only a few hours ago after you told me about the woman, and we talked about it, you still had spirit; you had hope. Have you forgotten the resolution we made together? Hardly an hour gone?

WARDER: You there! Go away, I say.

BOY: He's a vicious one. How did we miss the fruitseller?

GIRL: Let's not bother with the fruitseller or the woman. Let's take stock of the situation.

BOY: What stock can we take?

GIRL: First. We have a gun in our hands.

BOY: Is it safe in your dress?

GIRL: Don't worry. We can't get the fruitseller.

BOY: That's obvious.

GIRL: We can't get the woman.

BOY: Don't I know that?

GIRL: But wait. Why did she tell you to give the bread to the fruitseller?

BOY: How should I know? I didn't ask her.

GIRL: It's obvious that there was an attempt to rescue Kimthhi. She told you about the raid in Ihururu. The gun was to have been given to Kimathi.

BOY: Yes . . . yes.

GIRL: It's only that something went wrong. So what do we do?

BOY: That is the question.

GIRL: Let's carry out the plan ourselves. We must rescue Kimathi.

BOY: Are you crazy?

GIRL: But we must! We must! You talked about the call. This is the call that the woman was talking to you about.

BOY: Yes. The call. And she said it as if . . . as if she was challenging something inside me. She said: one day you'll understand that beating those in your lot is not how to become a man. Yes. Yes. Let's rescue Kimathi. But how?

GIRL: We buy bread. We put the gun inside there. We bring it to the Warder. He gives the loaf to Kimathi. Kimathi shoots his way out of prison.

WARDER: You are still there! Stop capering and dancing about.

BOY: He's a vicious one, I tell you. Let's run away and plan how to do it, then come back . . . but he'll recognize us.

GIRL: Simple. We shall come back tomorrow morning disguised.

WARDER: [*coming toward them*]: I'll shoot you or lock you in. [*They run off*]: This prisoner . . . bad blood . . . . Since I came on duty, I have not yet rested. People . . . in and out . . . and the prisoner, tucked four well-guarded gates inside. If I were them, I would not bother with a trial. Just get the neck—

Enter woman as fruitseller.

WARDER: Hey! You fruitseller.

WOMAN: Oranges cheap to-day. Do you want to buy one?

WARDER: There's a boy and a girl looking for you.

WOMAN: A boy and a girl? Were . . . were they carrying anything in their hands?

WARDER: No. Nothing. Why?

WOMAN: Which way did they go?

WARDER: The way you just came.

WOMAN: It does not matter. Tell me Mr. Warder. Where's the warder who used to be here before you? I came earlier today and I saw he wasn't here.

WARDER: How do I know? Everything is upside down. We are all new here. Since yesterday. They keep on making sudden changes of guards. Between you and me, it's this prisoner Kimathi . . . bad blood *kabisa*. They fear there could be an armed rescue. Last night, his men with their bugles attacked Ihururu. Bad blood . . . if I were them, I would. . . .

[*helps himself to some oranges. Takes a coin out of his pocket.*]

WOMAN: Don't pay. Maybe when I come back?

[*goes out.*]

Fourth Trial

It is dark in the cell where Kimathi is seated at his accustomed corner, craning to catch some light through a tiny barbed wire window. He

53

is quietly, peacefully humming a freedom song tune and at the same time thinking deeply, when he hears aggressive footsteps, accompanied by whistling outside his cell. Guards outside the cell give a loud salute and Shaw Henderson walks past them. He is flanked by Waitina and two armed KAR soldiers. 1st and 2nd soldier. Kimathi does not turn to acknowledge their entry.

HENDERSON: [*giving orders to one of the guards*]: Fungua. Pesi. I want to pay my last respects to Prime Minister Sir Dedan Kimathi.

The guards and the second soldier laugh foolishly. First soldier wears a sad, serious face. The door is unbolted and Henderson enters arrogantly, provocatively.

HENDERSON: [*ironically*] Well, are you in a better frame of mind to-day, Field Marshal?

KIMATHI: Never experienced greater calm [*still looking away from him*]: Your envoys have wiped the mist from my eyes. Yes, I have a clear, clear vision. I see—

HENDERSON: Wake up Kimathi. Stop dreaming.

KIMATHI: [*turning round to face Henderson, fury in his eyes*]: What more do you want from me?
Sale of our people . . . land . . . sale of my soul.
For a badge from King George, or is it the Queen?
[*firmly*]: Shaw Henderson! Trader with people's lives!
[*Waitina makes to strike him, but Henderson checks him. Kimathi proceeds unperturbed*]: Yes, self-appointed saviour of our people. Listen and listen well. I will fight to the bitter end. Protect our soil. Protect our people. This is what I, Kimathi wa Wachiuri, swore at initiation.

HENDERSON: It will have to be from the hangman's rope, Mr. Field Marshal.

KIMATHI: Already sentenced, am I? How is that for even handed British justice!
[*laughs loudly, scornfully.*]

HENDERSON: [*maddened by Kimathi catching him at his own slip*]: Listen, you crazy madman. I am not taking any more sauciness from a stinking Mau Mau terrorist. Do you hear?

[*Kimathi looks at him, unmoved, proud*]:

I have done my very best to save you. This democratic government has stretched its patience to limits. But you are obviously beyond rescue. You play it rough, so you'll get it rough.

KIMATHI: Spare your threats for some other coward. You are wasting your breath.

HENDERSON: [*hysterically*]: Shut up! Or I will shoot you dead in this very cell. For the last time, Kimathi, where is Mathenge?

KIMATHI: [*chuckling scornfully*]: What am I supposed to say? Aah, out there! In the Forests of Nyandarua or Kirinyaga. Fighting you. Or shall I go up in one of your aeroplanes shouting: Surrender! Surrender! Surrender!

HENDERSON: [*infuriated*]: One more chance and watch it now, man. Where is Stanley Mathenge?

KIMATHI: [*defiantly*]: The second last chance? Yes. British justice. Look, it is no use, Shaw Hender . . .

HENDERSON: [*hysterically slaps him . . . once, twice*]: Askari!

2ND SOLDIER: [*saluting exaggeratedly in panic*]: Fande!

Kimathi laughs a loud, scornful laugh. He pierces the soldier with fiery eyes and then spits in disgust.

KIMATHI: Rats!

HENDERSON: [*slaps him again*]:

This is not your forest kingdom! Remember that.

KIMATHI: [*staring at him with eyes burning with fury*]: If you are a fighter, unfetter me now. Let us face each other. Man to man. Let us see which wrestler fells the other, you coward.

Now really wild, Shaw Henderson strikes him again and again, using hands, legs, gun and swearing as he strikes.

KIMATHI: [*obstinately*]: Go on, Shaw Henderson. Lash on, slave driver. [*suddenly Kimathi loses his temper and struggles to break his chains*]: Bullying coward! Did any of your kind ever fight an even-handed clean battle?

HENDERSON: [*stampedes out of the cell, shouting at the top of his voice*]: Right askari! Remove him to the torture chamber and let Gatotia give him intensive treatment.

[*bullying the soldiers who remain behind in the cell as he and Waitina march off to the torture chamber*]: Haraka!

SECOND SOLDIER: Ndiyo, Afande! [*He roughs Kimathi up as they lead him to the torture chamber*]:

FIRST SOLDIER: [*maddened by the violence, whispers to his companion*]: Are you a human being? What are you doing this for?

The second soldier turns angrily as if to respond and then moves on behind Kimathi. But the roughing up stops.

HENDERSON: [*seen from next-door—in the torture chamber*]: Bastard black native. This oath has gone into their heads. [*In a commanding voice*]: Ready boys? Right, Gatotia, set to work. Bwana Waitina will instruct you when to do what.

WAITINA: [*With great appetite*]: Don't you worry! I'll do it myself. [*Addressing Kimathi*]: Lie down here.

Waitina ceremoniously folds up his shirt sleeves and feels an enormous whip with tremendous appetite. Gatotia and the Second Soldier remove Kimathi's shirt roughly and lay him on the floor, still fettered. As Waitina lifts the whip lights go off and the audience only hear noise from the torture chamber. Gradually, semi-darkness. In semi-darkness we watch the miming of black history (earlier enacted) going on, against the torturing behind the scene. There should be as much harmony as possible between the action on the visible stage and the goings on in the torture chamber.

WAITINA: [*whipping and questioning simultaneously*]: Where is Mathenge? [*whip, whip, whip*]: Where in your wild jungles is Stanley Mathenge? [*whip*]: Matenjagwo? [*whip*]: Where?

[*Whip*]: Where? Speak. [*Kimathi groans with pain*]: Okay, he wants to talk. Leave off Gatotia. Let him talk.

KIMATHI: [*to Gatotia*]: What medal are you working for, traitor! Cursed vermin!

WAITINA: Continue, Gatotia! Teach him how to curse. [*whip, whip, whip, whip whip*]: Stop Gatotia. Ready to talk now, Field Marshal? [*Kimathi continues to groan*]; Gatotia!

GATOTIA: Sir!

WAITINA: Hardcore's electric treatment now.

GATOTIA: Yes Sir!

WAITINA: [*slapping Kimathi*]: Where are Mathenge, Matenjagwo and the remaining terrorists? [*slap*]: Sign this letter and tell them to surrender.

KIMATHI: *That* I will never do.

WAITINA: All right then. I will show you . . . [*Groaning from the torture chamber. Waitina swears, abuses and shouts at Kimathi as the job goes on.*]

Kimathi, blood-stained, shirt torn, emerges from the torture chamber kicked, pushed from behind. He can hardly walk. He falls on his hands and feet. Henderson, Waitina and Gatotia and the two soldiers follow, holding some of the instruments of torture. They stand in a group except the human soldier who stands apart, slightly hiding his face in shame. Kimathi is obviously broken in body . . . BUT not in spirit.

HENDERSON: Now sign. [*Silence.*]
Sign—surrender.

He throws the piece of paper at Kimathi. It falls on the floor. Kimathi struggles to rise and now addresses himself to Gatotia and the soldiers.

KIMATHI: [*speaking in pain*]:
You . . . traitors to your people . . .
sellers of your own people . . . . For what?

Your own stomachs. A seat at the master's
table. A bank account. A partnership in
business. Partnership? To rob your people . . .
murder your people . . . for . . . medals and
leftovers! Our people will never forget you, fat traitors.
[*he takes the piece of paper*]:
This, Henderson . . . . (*Pause*)
For four hundred years the oppressor
has exploited and tortured our people.
For four hundred years we have risen
and fought against oppression,
against humiliation,
against enslavement of body
Mind and soul
[*tearing the piece of paper*]:
Our people will never surrender!
[*throws the pieces in Henderson's face.*]
HENDERSON: Gatotia! Soldiers! Take him.
Back to the chamber.

THIRD MOVEMENT

Street in Nyeri, the following day

Another Dawn. Early morning light. Bird whistles.
Enter Boy and Girl dressed as Maasai. They walk to the gate of
the jail house.

WARDER: Simama nyinyi! What do you want?
BOY: We want to see the prisoner?
WARDER: [*roughly*]: Which prisoner? Go away. This is not a Maasai
    manyatta.
BOY: But, the prisoner is there . . . Kimathi.

WARDER: Wonders will never cease. Maasai? Kimathi? Who are you fooling? Go away!

GIRL: We only want to greet him. And give him this loaf of bread.

WARDER: Bread for Kimathi? Here, bring it. Moran, what is your connection with Kimathi? Fighters, eh? Warriors. All night I've been here without food, not a bite. Thank you for the bread.

BOY AND GIRL: It's not for you!

Suddenly there's a sound of motorcycles starting, police sirens, planes in the sky.

VOICE: Liprightlipright . . . attention!

We hear steps of marching feet. They sound as if they are coming to the gate. Warder throws the loaf onto the ground. Boy and Girl rush to get it. Then they stand aside and look at the sky. Sound of aeroplanes. There is a shout off the stage. They run out. Enter woman from one side, still dressed as a fruitseller. Immediately Boy and Girl enter from another side. They knock into one another.

BOY AND GIRL: [*surprised*]: Fruitseller! [*they whisper in a corner*].

WOMAN: Oranges cheap today—
   Why, it's Maasai,
   In Nyeri!

GIRL: [*approaching*]: Excuse me, Mr. Fruitseller.

WOMAN: Yes.

GIRL: We were sent to give you bread—[*woman suddenly recognizes the Boy and Girl and she laughs, revealing herself.*]

WOMAN: Wonders will never cease! I would not have recognized you.

BOY AND GIRL: It's the woman!

WOMAN: Sssssssch! Follow me to a corner where we can talk.

They move a little way off. Both Girl and Boy sit at the feet of the woman. It should be symbolic: the woman now represents all the working mothers talking to their children.

WOMAN: We shall sit here where we can see them take him away. You still have the bread?

BOY: Why did you trick me into carrying a gun?

WOMAN: So you found out? I thought you told me you were ready for initiation. Son, I told you, you are a man and no longer a child. I shall not accept less of you. We cannot accept less of our youth. Were you afraid?

GIRL: He was! He was!

BOY: I was ... but the Girl here .... She was all strength and daring and no fear.

WOMAN: [*proud*]: That is the way it should always be. Instead of fighting against one another, we who struggle against exploitation and oppression, should give one another strength and faith till victory is ours.

GIRL: [*despondently*]: It is hard. It is hard seeing that we are weak.

WOMAN: United, our strength becomes the faith that moves mountains.

BOY: Why did you come upon us so suddenly and also disguised?

WOMAN: In the struggle, you learn to adapt to changed circumstances. Yesterday was a day of setbacks. First the screening and the Johnnies! I walked into the mouth of a gun! Then, after we parted, I found out that the fruitseller was among the ones picked in yesterday's morning raid. That was a crucial contact gone. This upset all the plans. What was I to do? I dressed as a fruitseller so that you would easily recognize me. The court adjourned sooner than I had thought: I then followed the crowd. I was going to speak to the Warder, another contact. I found that he too had been transferred to another place. So only you remained. I kept on looking for you. Between here and Majengo, there is not a place I have not visited. Great risks: but the task once started must be completed.

GIRL: What are you now going to do? You, alone?

WOMAN: [*contemplating Boy and Girl*]: I am not alone. You are there!

GIRL: [*jumping up—excited—proudly*]: I am ready!

BOY: [*also jumping up*]: I too am ready! But what shall we do?

WOMAN: [*thoughtfully*]: Listen. Kimathi is a genius in this struggle. It is therefore important to rescue him even at the cost of a few lives. The struggle must continue. They'll soon take him to court. I shall first go in, dressed to kill. Then you'll follow dressed as you are: I will speak to Kimathi with my eyes. When I cough, you start shooting. In the confusion, Dedan will follow me. An unexpected surprise can do miracles. Once five fighters made a whole Homeguard post surrender. It's all a matter of timing. Thereafter it's luck: we make our way to Majengo. Once there, none can find us.

BOY: [*excited*]; Trrrrrrrr! Trrrrrrrrrrr!

GIRL: Trrrrrrrrr! [*they mime a shoot out. Then the Girl suddenly loses interest in the game. She turns to the woman*]: Who really is Dedan Kimathi?

WOMAN: Leader of the landless. Leader of them that toil.

BOY: [*also catching the doubt in the Girl*]: How do we really know that it is Kimathi that they have arrested and not another person?

GIRL: I myself do not believe it! Because Kimathi would have known of the arrest and escaped in time. I have heard of the story of how once he wrote a letter to the Governor. He said he would dine with the Governor at State House. The Governor collected all the police in Nairobi to come and capture Kimathi. But Kimathi went there. He was disguised as a European Inspector of Police. Later, he wrote another letter to the Governor: Thank you for your dinner last night. And it was signed: F/Marshal D.K.

BOY: I have also heard it said that he could turn himself into an aeroplane. And also that before an attack on a garrison, he himself would go and blow a bugle from the inside.

GIRL: That he could walk for a 100 miles on his belly—

BOY: That in the forest, he could laugh and no enemy would hear him.

GIRL: That he could mimic any noise of a bird and none could tell the difference—

BOY: How then could they arrest him?

GIRL: They have caught his shadow.

WOMAN: [*sadly, contemplatively*]: It is true children, that Kimathi could do many things. Even today, they sing of the battle of Mathari; the battles he waged in Mount Kenya; the battle of Naivasha. Yes, they sing of the enemy aeroplanes he brought down with only a rifle! He was a wonderful teacher: with a laugh that was truly infectious. He could also act and mimic any character in the world: a story teller too, and many were the nights he would calm his men and make their hearts light and gay with humorous anecdotes. But above all, he loved people, and he loved his country. He so hated the sight of Africans killing one another that he sometimes became a little soft with our enemies. [*softly*]: He, Great commander that he was, Great organiser that he was, Great fearless fighter that he was, he was human! [*almost savagely, bitterly*]: Too human at times!

Nyandarua Forest: A Guerilla Camp

As the woman finishes the last words the scene suddenly changes to a court-cum-general meeting in the forest. We now see a crowd of forest fighters enter the stage, singing the song of Kimathi.

"Rwimbo Rwa Kimathi":

When our Kimathi ascended
Into the mountain alone
He asked for strength and courage
To defeat the whiteman

He said that we should tread
The paths that he had trodden
That we should follow his steps
And drink from his cup of courage

If you drink from this cup of courage
The cup that I have drunk from myself
It is a cup of pain and sorrow
A cup of tears and death and freedom. . . .

Enter Kimathi followed by other generals: Njama, Matenjagwo, Mbaria Kahiu, Kimemia, Ole Kisio, etc. and the woman. They are all simply dressed and carry themselves with dignity.

KIMATHI: Njama!

NJAMA: Marshal!

KIMATHI: Take up your pen [*turning to Matenjagwo*]: Matenjagwo, Ole Kisio!

OLE KISIO AND MATENJAGWO: Marshal!

KIMATHI: Have you placed guards on every side?

OLE KISIO: Yes, Field Marshal.

MATENJAGWO: Over a two mile radius. All the strategic places.

KIMATHI: Kimbo! Mbaria!

MBARIA & KIMBO: Marshal!

KIMATHI: Bring the murderers.
Bring the mercenaries.

Commotion. Two British soldiers and one African K.A.R. are brought in, hands bound behind them.

KIMATHI: [*to the British soldiers*]: Your regiment?

1ST & 2ND BRITISH SOLDIERS: Lincoln Fusiliers.

KIMATHI: Your names?

1ST SOLDIER: Winterbottom!

2ND SOLDIER: Smith!

KIMATHI: From where?

1ST BRITISH SOLDIER: Scotland . . . Dundee.

2ND BRITISH SOLDIER: Southampton, Great Britain.

KIMATHI: Wealthy parents or workers?

SOLDIERS: Poor. We are poor.
Just working people.

KIMATHI: Are you fighting for the working people of your country?

SOLDIERS: [*They look at one another, confused, as if they don't know what he is talking about.*]

KIMATHI: It's always the same story. Poor men sent to die so that parasites might live in paradise with ill-gotten wealth. Know that we are not fighting against the British people. We are fighting against British colonialism and imperialist robbers of our land, our factories, our wealth. Will you denounce British imperialism?

SOLDIERS: [*standing up straight, trying to muster dignity*]:
We are the Queen's soldiers!

KIMATHI: [*angry*]: This kind of imperialism's vermin
Makes my blood boil with hate.
Did you come all this way
Many thousands of miles
Across the sea, over the air,
Along way from you home,
To kill our people
So that Lord So-and-So
Might drink other people's blood in peace?

1ST SOLDIER: We were only obeying orders—

KIMATHI: To kill—

CROWD: Kill them
Hang imperialist agents!

KIMATHI: [*contemptuous disgust*]: Out vermin!
Take them away.
[*turning to the African, after the others are taken out*]:
And you—
You look like one of us.

KAR SOLDIER: Truly. I'm black. Black like you. Spare me brother.

KIMATHI: And yet you fight against us?
A true mercenary!
You fought for imperialism in Burma!
You fought for them in Japan!

And now you fight for them
Against your own country?
Against your people's interest!
How much do they give you?

KAR SOLDIER: One hundred shillings.

KIMATHI: A month? Is that all?

KAR SOLDIER: Plus posho!

KIMATHI: [laughs]: Only that?

KAR SOLDIER: Only that!

KIMATHI: And for only that
You kill your people?
I thought they would bribe you with more!
A share in their motor companies.
A share in their Export-Import trade,
A share in their Tourist hotels,
A share in their wheat fields
A share in their stolen wealth.
Only that?
And for a hundred shillings
And posho
And a medal
You help them murder,
You help them massacre,
You help them plunder?
You are ready to die
In the pay of imperialists?

Offstage: a burst of machine gun fire from the firing squad.

KAR SOLDIER: [*frightened*]: Forgive me, brother.

KIMATHI: [*sadly*]: Take him away.
[*ferociously*]: Take the mercenary away.

He is led out protesting.

KIMATHI: Vigilance!

There is another firing squad and a scream.

KIMATHI: Vigilance. We must be vigilant all the time
Welcome once again warriors and comrades
To the last day of our meeting.
For three days now
We have debated many issues
That affect the conduct
And the growing strength
Of our Movement.
Since we formed our six brave armies:
Ituma Ndemi Army
Gikuyu Iregi Army
Kenya Inoro Army
Mei Mathathi Army
Townwatch Battalions
Kenya Levellation Army,
We have had great victories.
Our enemies all over Kenya
Have not been able to sleep.
That now they have called in
Their best Generals:
Lathbury, Hinde, Erskine
And also
Their latest fighter bombers
Shows that we have hit them
Where it hurts most.
We now must open new fronts
We have sent envoys to arouse
Warriors from Nyanza,
Giriama people at the Coast
And also young Kalenjin braves,
To set a grand alliance of Kenyan People
And chastise the enemy for ever.

We have also sent emissaries to Ethiopia
To see if we can get a supply of Arms.
But I must continue to stress
That first and foremost
We must rely on our strength
As the most conscious,
The best organized fighting arm
of the Kenyan People.
We must continue to make more guns
I want to see every warrior with a gun
Hand grenades
Machine guns
Molotov cocktails.
Every camp, every mbuci, should have
its own factory.
We now have excellent blacksmiths
Who can make guns and machine guns
So you can't tell the difference between
Ours and those captured from the enemy.
Start clothing factories:
We have excellent material
From barks of trees and skins of animals.
Put more effort in education:
This earth will form our blackboards
We must know our history
Especially the deeds of those
Who have always resisted
The rape of our beautiful Kenya
Who have always stood firmly
Against oppression and exploitation.
I could sing praise for them all day:
Waiyaki, Me Katilili
Mbatiani, Koitalel.
And villify collaborators:
Mumias, Wangombe
Karuri, Gakure

Kinyanjui, Luka—
All who sold us to foreigners to aid
their own stomachs and their family store.
We must learn from our past strength
Past weaknesses
From past defeats
And past victories.
Also clear a few farms to grow grain
Here in the Forest
Where we have even made friends with
Birds and snakes and animals
So that they even warn us
About enemies approaching.
Here we must plant seeds for a
future society
Here in the forest armed in body
mind and soul
We must kill the lie
That black people never invented anything
Lay for ever to rest that inferiority
complex
Implanted in our minds by centuries
of oppression.
Rise, Rise workers and peasants of Kenya
Our victory is the victory of the working
people
The victory of all those in the world
Who to-day fight and struggle for total
liberation.
Long live Kenya People's Defence Council!

ALL: Long live Kenya People's Defence Council!

KIMATHI: [*change of tone*]:
Bring the offenders
Internal enemies of our cause!
[*while people go out to fetch them, Kimathi continues with his speech*]:

The enemies of our people are strong
They have the bombers
They have machinegun fire
Their striking power is awesome
Why should I hide that from you?
They have greater and more efficient
Weapons of propaganda.
The radio, newspapers, schools,
Their universities where they give
Our children
An education to enfeeble minds,
Make them slaves, apes, parrots
Shadows of the men and women
they could have been.
But they are also weak,
Very weak, the famed giant
on mosquito legs.
Our love of freedom is our bullet
Our successes are our newspaper
But
Stronger than any machinegun fire
Stronger than the Lincoln and
Harvard bombers
Mightier than their best generals
Is our unity and discipline in struggle
With unity, discipline
Along correct lines
People's line
With unity and discipline
In our total commitment to
The liberation of us
who sweat and labour
We can move mountains
We can yet cut off the giant's
legs and mammoth head
Truth is our atomic bomb

But
Discipline is our hydrogen bomb
ALL: Long live People's Field Marshal
Long live Kenyan People's Freedom Armies!

Kimathi is in a kind of trance. He stares beyond them, into the distance. Mbaria approaches him.

MBARIA: Marshal!
KIMATHI: There are others:
Those who went to negotiate
with the enemy despite the ban
on talks at this stage
of our struggle.
Know you that our Movement
is facing a crucial test:
One faction is advocating selling out
And negotiating
Creating a new colony
Where we shall be mere pawns.
We must denounce them!
We must fight them out
And root out the trend
In our midst.

ALL: Long live Kenya People's Defence Council!
Long live Kenyan People's Freedom Armies!

Hungu, Gati, Gaceru, are brought in. Then after a small interval, Wambararia, Kimathi's brother is brought in in chains. Kimathi is looking away from them. Slowly he turns round. His eyes fall on those of his younger brother, Wambararia.

KIMATHI: [*shocked*]: Wambararia! [*Pause*]: Even you, my brother?
WAMBARARIA: I am . . . I was . . . .

70

KIMATHI: My kindred brother—

> To negotiate behind my back?
> [*he sits down*]: Kimemia—speak.

KIMEMIA: Marshal,

> I agree with you about discipline
> Self discipline.
> Group discipline.
> Physical and mental discipline.
> Political and military discipline.
> We are our people in arms.
> Time and time again
> You have told us
> There is time for talk
> Time for criticism
> Time for self-criticism.
> That has been our way.
> [*turning to the crowd*]:
> Has Kimathi ever prevented a brother
> From speaking his mind?

CROWD: Noooooooooooooooo!

KIMEMIA: His motto has always been

> Talk
> Talk till agreement is reached
> But once rules have been set,
> Once tasks have been assigned,
> They must be obeyed
> Until, unless, the group revises
> Or reverses the rules and the tasks
> Not to do so
> Is to jeopardise our lives for nothing
> To sabotage our cause
> It is treason to the people
> It is like having homeguards
> In our midst!
> These traitors must die!

There is silence. Several hands are raised, other generals and fighters anxious to speak.

1ST GUERILLA FIGHTER: Forgive them.
    Although they have done this
    It's their first offence.
    To kill them will diminish
    Our number.
2ND GUERILLA FIGHTER: It's not numbers that fight
    Better fifty men
    Armed with faith
    Armed with discipline
    Than a thousand villains
    Doubters,
    Possible collaborators.
3RD GUERILLA FIGHTER: They have fought bravely
    In the past.
4TH GUERILLA FIGHTER: Past. Past. That is history.
    We should learn from our past.
    But it would be a great mistake
    To become its slaves!
    Must we let songs
    Of a patriotic past
    Betray the needy present?
    Must we let a past performance
    Be the basis on which
    We are sold to imperialism?
    How dare these negotiate our surrender?
5TH GUERILLA FIGHTER: One is Kimathi's brother.
    A kinsman.
    You cannot . . .
    The blood might turn against us
    And cry for vengeance from the earth.
KIMATHI: [*pointing to the woman. Talks contemplatively as if agitated within*]:
    Do you see this woman?

How many tasks has she performed
Without complaint
Between here and the villages?
How many people has she
snatched from jails, from colonial
Jaws of death!
How many brave warriors has she
recruited at great risks!
Walking for miles
Hardly getting sleep
for days.
When this struggle is over
We shall erect at all the city corners
Monuments
To our women
Their courage and dedication
To our struggle
Come forward, mother of people
Teach us a lesson on
Diligence and commitment
What do you say about
These slumberers?
These surrenderers of our freedom?

WOMAN: [*looks at Kimathi. Then she starts slowly working herself
into a passion as if trying to still the doubt wavering in Kimathi's
heart*]:

I want to say a word
In answer to what our brother
Has said about our kinsman!
Brother, Uncle, kinsman, clansman . . .
When will you learn?
We shall continue to suffer
Until that day
We can recognize our own
Our true kinsmen
When we can correctly

Identify our enemies
What is this superstitition about
Kindred blood even when it
turns sour and treacherous
to our long cherished cause?
My clansman, my kinsman,
My brother, my sister
If these are of my house
Let them honour
the oath of unity
Let them uphold
the struggle for liberation
from slavery, exploitation.
So whatever decision we make
It must be wise in itself
It must advance our struggle
And not be made on the basis
of kindred blood.

CROWD: Long live Kenya People's Defence Council
Long live Kenya People's struggle!

Silence.

KIMATHI: [*waking up from his contemplative position*]:
You Hungu—
What have you to say?

HUNGU: It's a first offence. Forgive me.

GACERU: It's a first offence. Forgive me.

GATI: It's a first offence. Forgive me.

MWENDANDA: We had only wanted to find out
What the many had to say.

6TH GUERILLA FIGHTER: They are all guilty.
But give them new tasks.
New commands.
If they fail to do them—

KIMEMIA: [*angry*]:
　　Then they will run away to the enemy
　　I've seen the glint in their eyes.
　　They will betray us
　　Should they do another wrong
　　For fear of people's wrath
　　For fear of people's justice.

KIMATHI: And you Wambararia
　　What have you to say?

They face one another. There is total silence.

WAMBARARIA: I too have heard the news.
　　I too know the terrible news.

KIMATHI: [*turns away, pained*]: Leave me alone. All of you.

All go out. Except the woman. Kimathi remains in the same position.

WOMAN: I know it pains.

KIMATHI: You don't know.

WOMAN: Your father
　　He was killed
　　In the first world war.

KIMATHI: [*reminiscing*]:
　　I was only a baby
　　But I've heard
　　He was respected in all
　　Karunaini.
　　A brave man.
　　Fell to German fire at Tanga.
　　But that's not all.

WOMAN: Your brother
　　Your elder brother
　　He was killed in the
　　Battle of Mathari!
　　He died for our cause.

KIMATHI: Norman.
　　Gichuhi.
　　A brave death.
　　Fighting for Kenya people's freedom.
　　I'll always remember him.
　　But that's not all.
WOMAN: I know.
　　Only your sister is left, true,
　　But that's the meaning of your choice.
KIMATHI: My choice.
　　Our choice.
　　Kindred blood
　　Blood of my blood.
　　We used to play with him
　　In Karunaini
　　In Theng'era stream
　　Exploring Kabage Forest
　　Sometimes running up to Mathari Hill
　　And we dreamed of Nyeri plains
　　And we made up stories about Mount Kenya.
　　Once when my finger was cut
　　Out there in the saw mill
　　It was Wambararia
　　Who tied it with a cloth.
　　Tearing his new shirt into shreds
　　Aah,
　　It pains.
　　I don't deny that
　　But
　　That's not all.

He takes out a letter and throws it at her...

KIMATHI: This was the letter
　　You brought me.
　　This was the terrible news

Contained in a piece of paper
You brought from Muhoya
Wambararia must have read it
And found out that
Mother is now crazy
That she collects flowers
And keeps on singing
Calling on God
To spare Wambararia,
To spare her youngest—

Silence—woman hands back the letter.

WOMAN: It pains the woman in me too!
Thinking of the past,
And the dear ones we left behind
Can weaken our resolve.
You are a leader of
A revolution.
You must decide.
But remember
All the others
Have left their wives,
Their children,
Their mothers,
Behind.
KIMATHI: [*walks about the stage*]:
Go!
Call them.
Call them back.

They all stream back.

KIMATHI: [*resolutely*]:
Friends.
Comrades in struggle.

It's their first offence.
It is a serious offence.
But we shall not
Give the hyena twice!
They'll not be killed today.
But they'll be caned
And kept without food
For three days.
We shall keep a close watch
On all of them.
Watch all their activities.
We must re-educate them
Into new resolves.
But should they repeat a similar act
Should they even dare—

*Some cheer; others seem resentful about the decision. They all go
out. Kimathi remains on the stage.*

KIMATHI: Organisation,
Vigilance,
Discipline.
Something strange rubs me
Under the skin . . .
My mother . . . .

*Kimemia comes onto the stage running; followed by the woman
at a distance.*

KIMEMIA: Marshal! Marshal!
KIMATHI: Speak.
KIMEMIA: Wambararia
Mwendanda
Gati
All
They have run away
They have escaped.

KIMATHI: [*silence. Then becomes suddenly decisive*]:
Follow them to the valley.
Tell Matenjagwo
Ole Kisio
To run to Mugumoini
And to the other crossing.
Shoot them on sight!

Courtroom

Courtroom. But now the white people's side is joined by Politician, Business Executive, Priest, Banker, Gati, Gatotia, Hungu, Gaceru, Mwendanda— who occupy a bench at the very back and not proper chairs like the whites.
The judge is in the chair.
Kimathi is still in chains and heavily guarded as in the former court scene.

JUDGE: You have been charged that on the night of Sunday, October the 21st, 1956, at or near Ihururu in Nyeri District, you were found in possession of a firearm, namely a revolver, without a licence contrary to Special Emergency Regulations—a contravention that constitutes a criminal offence. [*Kimathi stares at the collaborators*]: We have a lawyer to defend the accused. . . .

KIMATHI: Lawyers, Liars, Bankers, Owners of Property.

JUDGE: Without wasting time—

KIMATHI: Time is money. Money is justice.
Justice is money. Moneyed justice.
Thirty pieces of silver.
Judases. Traitors.

JUDGE: Those?
They have come to testify
the truth
How dictatorial you were
How depraved

How ruthless
Ruling your people through fear!

KIMATHI: Truth from slaves of injustice
Murderers of Truth.

JUDGE: Truth is truth. Just like
$2 + 2 = 4$.

KIMATHI: $2 + 2 = 4$? It depends on your base.

JUDGE: You tremble. Scared of
Justice and Truth?

KIMATHI: Scared? SCARED! CAST OUT THIS DOUBT. CAST
OUT . . . THIS DOUBT.

Enter woman, dressed like a lady. Kimathi recognizes her immediately. There is sudden re-assurance in his department. Woman looks at Kimathi. Their eyes meet. Judge watches the woman intently.

The woman is making her way to a seat when general unrest develops from the back, on the side of the whites. She squeezes in among other blacks, somewhere near the front. The commotion at the back takes momentum as Gatotia, Gaceru, Gati, Hungu and Mwendanda confer together with lowered heads, whispering excitedly and throwing quick, anxious glances at the woman. All this takes place in a matter of seconds.

JUDGE: [*banging on the table*]:
Order in the court!

Silence.

JUDGE: May everyone here present note that the accused has dismissed voluntary legal advice placed at his disposal by the Government. I am, therefore, left with no alternative but to proceed with prosecution, taking the accused to be his own defender. I will now repeat the charge for the very last time. The accused is advised to listen carefully and submit his plea.

As he is going through the above pronouncement, the collaborators grow even busier and more panicky. Gaceru whispers to Gatotia who in turn alerts a white police officer, seated in a comfortable chair, next to the corridor, in the row immediately ahead of them. The officer immediately rises and walks towards the woman, beckoning Gatotia to follow by wagging a finger at him. Gatotia obeys. They lead the woman out but she hesitates directly opposite the dock to look at Kimathi who looks at her. She is pushed out of the courtroom where Gatotia chains her. As she is taken away, she breaks into triumphant singing (freedom song), flooding the courtroom with her powerful, militant voice. There is whispering and general excitement in the court.

All this happens within forty or so seconds. Certainly in no more than a minute.

SONG:
> Bururi uyu witu
> Andu Airu
> Ngai ni aturathimiire
> Na akiuga tutikoima kuo.

Boy and girl enter—not in disguise. They squeeze into the space just vacated by the woman. The Woman's militant song continues to flood the courtroom. The judge pretends to be busy giving orders to the clerk but he is really only killing an uncomfortable minute. Kimathi watches the Boy and Girl until they take their seats.

JUDGE: [*with pretended confidence*]: Silence in court! Will the guards at the court entrance ensure that no more latecomers are allowed into the courtroom. It is creating unnecessary commotion. [*African Guards salute stiffly, obediently*]:
Dedan Kimathi s/o Wachiuri, you are charged that on the night of Sunday, October the 21st, 1956, at or near Ihururu in Nyeri District, you were found in possession of a firearm, namely a revolver, without a licence, contrary to Section 89 of the Penal Code. Under Special Emergency Regulations, this

81

contravention constitutes a criminal offence. Guilty or not guilty?

Silence.

Kimathi stares at Hungu, Gati, Mwendanda and Gaceru. They look down or away, in shame.

JUDGE: Kimathi s/o Wachiuri, you have been found guilty of possessing a firearm which was found on your person at or near Ihururu on the night of October the 21st, contrary to Special Emergency Regulations. Have you anything to say before the sentence?

KIMATHI: In the court of Imperialism!
There has never and will never be
Justice for the people
Under imperialism.
Justice is created
through a revolutionary struggle
Against all the forces of imperialism.
Our struggle must therefore continue.
[*African people rise. Commotion. Police hold machine guns ready*]:
Don't walk into the mouth of guns
Unless you have yours organized!
[*resumes his speech*]:
In the forest, I was sometimes plagued
by doubts.
If I died today
Would our people continue
the struggle?
I would look at the braves
killed
I would say:
If I died to-day
Will this blood ever be

betrayed?
That was my Trial.
But now I know that
for every traitor
there are a thousand patriots.
[*pointing an accusing finger towards the collaborators' corner.
People automatically look there*]:
Signalled by Hungu, Gati,
Gaceru, Mwendanda and led by
Gatotia—the hooded Gakunia,
who has betrayed uncountable
sons and daughters of the soil,
[*astonishment from the blacks' side*]:
A servant of your imperialist law
only a while ago led out
A brave daughter of the soil,
A courageous patriot,
to the dungeons.
[*looking away from them in disgust and defiance*]:
But our people will never surrender
Internal and external foes
will be demolished
And Kenya shall be free!
[*applause from Africans*]:

JUDGE: Order in court!
KIMATHI: [*addressing the people*]:
So, go!
Organize in your homes
Organize in the mountains
Know that your only
Kindred blood is he
who is in the struggle
Denounce those who weaken
Our struggle
by creating ethnic divisions

Uproot from you those
Who are selling out to imperialism
Kenyan masses shall be free!

JUDGE: Kimathi s/o Wachiuri, you are sentenced to die, by hanging.
You will be hanged by the rope until you are dead.

KIMATHI: [*laughs.*]

*All rise. The judge leaves. The moment his robes are out of sight,
Boy and Girl, who have been all along restless, stand. Moving
swiftly toward Kimathi, Girl breaks the bread. Boy and Girl
simultaneously hold the gun.*

BOY AND GIRL: Not dead! [*the girl shakes her fists at guards.*]

*Utter commotion as a struggle between opposing forces ensues.
A loud shot is heard. Sudden darkness falls, but only for a
moment: for soon, the stage gives way to a mighty crowd of
workers and peasants at the centre of which are Boy and Girl,
singing a thunderous freedom song. All the soldiers are gone,
except for the First Soldier who shyly joins in the singing from
behind.*

People's Song and Dance:
Male and Female soloists recommended.

SOLOISTS: Ho-oo, ho-oo mto mkuu wateremka!
GROUP: Ho-oo, ho-oo mto mkuu wateremka!
SOLOISTS: Magharibi kwenda mashariki
GROUP: Mto mkuu wateremka
SOLOISTS: Kaskazini kwenda kusini
GROUP: Mto mkuu wateremka
SOLOISTS: Hoo-i, hoo-i kumbe adui kweli mjinga
GROUP: Hoo-i, hoo-i kumbe adui kweli mjinga
SOLOISTS: Akaua mwanza mimba wetu
GROUP: Akijitia yeye mshindi
SOLOISTS: Wengi zaidi wakazaliwa

GROUP: Tushangilie mazao mapya

SOLOISTS: Vitinda mimba marungu juu

GROUP: Tushambulie adui mpya.

SOLOISTS: Hoo-ye, hoo-ye wafanya kazi wa ulimwengu

GROUP: Hoo-ye, hoo-ye wafanyi kazi wa ulimwengu

SOLOISTS: Na wakulima wote wadogo

GROUP: Tushikaneni mikono sote

SOLOISTS: Tutwange nyororo za wabeberu

GROUP: Hatutaki utumwa tena.

SOLOISTS: Hoo-ye, hoo-ye umoja wetu ni nguvu yetu

GROUP: Hoo-ye, hoo-ye umoja wetu ni nguvu yetu

SOLOISTS: Tutapigana mpaka mwisho

GROUP: Tufunge vita na tutashinda

SOLOISTS: Majembe juu mapanga juu

GROUP: Tujikomboe tujenge upya.